HISTORIC SCOTLAND

# PICTS, GAELS AND SCOTS

*For Rod and my parents*

HISTORIC SCOTLAND

# PICTS, GAELS AND SCOTS

## Early Historic Scotland

SALLY M. FOSTER

B. T. Batsford Ltd / Historic Scotland

First published 1996
Reprinted with corrections 1997

Typeset by Bernard Cavender Design & Greenwood Graphics Publishing
and printed in Great Britain by The Bath Press, Bath

Published by B. T. Batsford Ltd
583 Fulham Road, London SW6 5BY

A CIP catalogue record for this book is available from
the British Library

ISBN 0 7134 7485 8 (cased)
0 7134 7486 6 (limp)

# Contents

# Illustrations

# Colour Plates

# Acknowledgements

Any overview of a subject is the sum of the knowledge and hard work of many people other than the author. I am therefore grateful to everyone whose published and unpublished works have formed the basis for my text, yet whose contribution cannot be fully acknowledged in either the text or short bibliography.

Numerous people have helped disguise the true extent of my ignorance, particularly Leslie Alcock and Dauvit Broun. Their original and stimulating research often helped shape my ideas, and they kindly read and commented on a first draft (for which final responsibility, including errors, rests with the author). I am also grateful to the following for their advice and assistance: Jonquil Alpe, Fionna Ashmore, John Barrett, Cormac Bourke, Jane Brann, Marilyn Brown, Jack Burt, Emma Carver, Anne Crone, Stephen Driscoll, Lesley Fergusson, Eric Fernie, Katherine Forsyth, Ian A. Fraser, Marion Fry, Bob Gourlay, Tom Gray, Jill Harden, Isabel Henderson, John Higgitt, Tim Holden, Fraser Hunter, John Hunter, Ronald Inglis, Alan Lane, Chris MacGregor, Kevin McLaren, Gordon Maxwell, Diane Nelson, Susan Payne, Edwina Proudfoot, Anna Ritchie, Graham Ritchie, Ross Samson, David Sanderson, Niall Sharples, Ian Shepherd, Alison Sheridan, Mike Spearman, Simon Taylor, Val Turner, Bruce Walker, Doreen Waugh, Mike Williams, John Wood, Alex Woolf and Historic Scotland colleagues.

With regard to illustrations, the staff of both the Royal Commission on the Ancient and Historical Monuments of Scotland (RCAHMS) and National Museum of Scotland (NMS) were particularly helpful. Tom Gray's pictures (**2** and **78**) were first published in E. Sutherland *In Search of the Picts* (London, 1994). Unless otherwise stated, the remaining pictures are Historic Scotland copyright. Dave Pollock drew **25, 30** and **colour plate** 8. Christina Unwin drew **1, 4, 7–8, 13–14, 22, 44, 46–7, 53, 56, 59, 64, 68, 84** and **88**. The summary of the ogham alphabet (**8**) is based on C. Thomas *And Shall These Mute Stones Speak?* (Cardiff, 1994), with amendments; (**14**) is based on Nicolaisen (1986) and B.E. Crawford *Scandinavian Scotland* (Leicester, 1987); (**38**) is based on Driscoll (1991) with additions; the distribution of imported pottery (**44**) is based on the illustration by E. Campbell in N. Edwards *The Archaeology of Early Medieval Ireland* (London, 1990), with additions and amendments; the distribution of *eccles*-place-names (**53**) is based on G.W.S. Barrow 'The childhood of Scottish Christianity', *Scottish Studies*, 27 (1983), A.S. Henshall 'A long cist cemetery at Parkburn Sand Pit, Lasswade, Midlothian', *Proc. Soc. Antiq. Scot.*, 89 (1955–6) and Thomas (1981) with additions; the plans of early Christian sites (**56** and **59**) are mainly based on RCAHMS *Argyll 2–5* (Edinburgh, 1975–84) and C. Thomas *The Early Christianity of North Britain* (Glasgow, 1971); the distribution of handbells (**64**) is based on C.

9

Bourke 'The hand-bells of the early Scottish church', *Proc. Soc. Antiq. Scot.*, 113 (1983), with additions.

Quotations from Bede's *Ecclesiastical History of the English People*, translated by Leo Sherley-Price and revised by R.E. Latham (Penguin Classics, 2nd rev. edn, 1990) are reproduced by kind permission of Penguin Books Ltd.

David Breeze encouraged me to write this and subsequently acted as a conscientious series editor. Peter Kemmis Betty, Monica Kendall and Charlotte Vickerstaff knocked it into shape and saw it through to production. Without the advice and continuous support of Rod McCullagh none of this would have been possible.

# Note on terminology

This is the *early* historic period and there is inevitably debate about the exact date of some events; spellings also vary. For the sake of consistency, Smyth's dating (1984) is adopted throughout. Unless stated otherwise, all dates are AD (after Christ).

The names used for both the past inhabitants of Scotland and their nations has varied through time, and are a close reflection of political circumstances. The historian Dauvit Broun (1994) suggests the following terminology (the reasoning for which is explained in greater detail in Chapters 1 and 7):

Argyll is used here to refer to the territory of people called the Dál Riata – Gaels who had originally come from Ireland. The native inhabitants of Scotland – the Picts – lived in 'Pictland' (a modern term of convenience since no contemporary name is known). The Dál Riata and Picts gradually amalgamated, but it is only from *c.* 900 that they would have recognized themselves as Scots, living in *Alba*.

Many of the places mentioned can be visited, and their location is shown at the back of the book (see **88**).

| Date | People | Place |
| --- | --- | --- |
| pre-900 | *Picti*/Picts | Pictland |
| | Dál Riata (*Scoti*/Gaels) | Argyll |
| 10th–13th centuries | Scots (Gaels) | *Alba* |

# CHAPTER ONE

# Setting the scene

Early historic Scotland, from the fifth to tenth centuries, was home to five different peoples and cultures: the Picts, Dál Riata (Gaels), Britons, Angles and latterly the Vikings. By the early eleventh century the first four of these were unified and Scotland had established a stable and successful monarchy. Geographically it extended south into modern England, while its western and northern fringes, including Caithness, were Norwegian. Since the tenth century, historians have tended to credit one man - Cináed mac Ailpín (Kenneth mac Alpin) - with laying the foundations of this modern Scottish nation. In about 842 this Gael rose to prominence as ruler of a united kingdom comprising both the Picts and Dál Riata. Yet, as we shall see, he was not the first individual to rule both countries simultaneously, and it was in fact the considerable achievements of the Picts which had laid the foundations for this. Their precocious legacy was to have both set the scene for and begun the process of consolidation of the Scottish kingdom. In fact the events of c. 900 are the more important landmark. At this point *Alba,* which had originally been the Gaelic word for Great Britain as a whole, was appropriated for Pictland by a new Scottish nation consciously attempting to break with the past. It did so by defining a new type of kingdom which could be expressed in terms of a territory as well as a people.

The key questions are therefore: when did this process of consolidation take place, and

why, how and where? There are no ready answers to these questions, but as we review the various strands of historical and archaeological evidence for the Picts and Dál Riata a clearer picture will begin to emerge.

## Who were the Picts?

Classical and later early historic sources use a variety of evolving terms to signify the people who inhabited Scotland and/or their territorial divisions prior to the late eighth century (**1**). Of these terms *Picti*, first recorded in 297 and derived from the Picts' own name for themselves, or possibly a Roman nickname meaning 'the painted ones', has been the most enduring. Then, as in later Classical sources, the Picts were referred to as assailants of the Roman frontier in Britain. Much ink has been spilt over what the ancient writers meant by Picts, but it seems to be a generic term for people living north of the Forth–Clyde isthmus who raided the Roman empire. There is a distinction in archaeological remains to north and south of the Forth–Clyde isthmus in the early centuries which would seem to support this definition, although some archaeologists argue that the cultural boundary lay further north, at the River Tay. The Picts seem to have been an amalgam of earlier tribes – as many as twelve were recorded by Ptolemy (an Alexandrian geographer) in the second century. Tacitus, the Roman historian, records that some of these

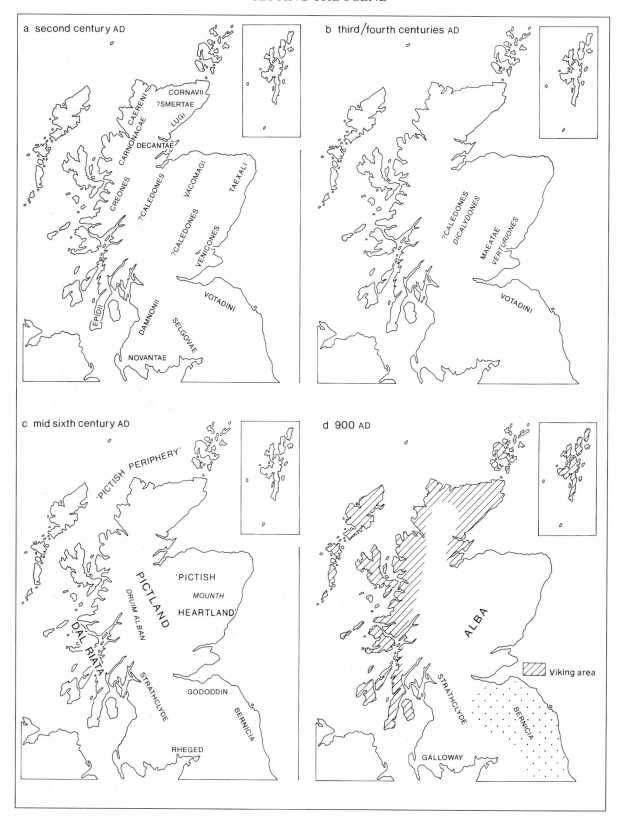

a second century AD

CORNAVII
?SMERTAE
CAERENI
LUGI
CARNONACAE
DECANTAE
CREONES
?CALEDONES
VACOMAGI
TAEXALI
?CALEDONES
VENICONES
EPIDII
DAMNONII
VOTADINI
SELGOVAE
NOVANTAE

b third/fourth centuries AD

?CALEDONES
DICALYDONES
MAEATAE
VERTURIONES
VOTADINI

c mid sixth century AD

'PICTISH PERIPHERY'
PICTLAND
'PICTISH
MOUNTH
HEARTLAND'
DRUIM ALBAN
DAL RIATA
STRATHCLYDE
GODODDIN
BERNICIA
RHEGED

d 900 AD

ALBA
Viking area
STRATHCLYDE
BERNICIA
GALLOWAY

**1** *The known names of tribes and kingdoms in Scotland between the first century and beginning of the tenth century. Precise locations are often difficult to define and fixed boundaries are unlikely to have existed. Nor can we be certain that the sources named all the existing peoples or completely understood what they were describing.*

tribes combined against the army of his father-in-law, Agricola, in 83 after the battle of Mons Graupius.

There need be no suggestion that they were a 'nation' or uniform people, indeed at least two main internal divisions are referred to: the Maeatae and Caledones of the late second/early third century, later the Caledonii and other Picts, who had become the Verturiones and

**2** *The Collessie stone: the early Picts as they depicted themselves (Tom Gray).*

Dicalydones by the mid-fourth century. We cannot even be sure that these were the sole inhabitants of the country. We also do not know the name the Picts might have used for themselves (if indeed they recognized the concept!). But we can be confident that they were simply the descendants of the native Iron Age tribes of Scotland, most of whom were never part of the Roman empire and even when they were, were only affected for short periods of time (**2**). The notion of the Picts having existed in Galloway is now recognized as a myth which arose out of a misunderstanding by medieval writers.

Therefore in historical terms the term Pictish might be applied to the period between 79, when the Romans advanced beyond the Forth–Clyde isthmus into Caledonia, and 842/900 when the mac Ailpín dynasty came to establish itself. In practical terms the Picts (and indeed Dál Riata) only become truly recognizable as archaeological and historical entities from the sixth century, and it is on this later period that we shall inevitably concentrate.

## Who were the Dál Riata?

The Dál Riata were Gaels who originally came from the Antrim tribe of the Dál Riata (in north-east Ireland) (**3**). Tradition has it that *c.* 500 one of their number (Fergus Mór mac Eirc) established a new kingdom in Argyll in response to rival dynastic pressures in Ireland. There is no archaeological evidence for such a migration over the short sea-crossing of the North Channel between Antrim and Kintyre. However, the distribution of prehistoric artefacts and similarities in certain monument types attest to a long tradition of contact between north-east Ireland and west Scotland from Neolithic times. At around 500 there is also evidence for Irish settlements being founded in south-west Scotland, north Wales, Cornwall and Devon. Fergus Mór mac Eirc may simply have been the first member of the Dál Riata royal family to rule from Scotland

3 The Book of Kells *(produced in Iona c. 780-806): the Dál Riata as they depicted themselves? (The Board of Trinity College Dublin.)*

such as the Anglo-Saxon takeover of southern and eastern Britain.

But, in fact, when the Classical authors and later early historic sources used the term *Scoti* (Scots) it had a completely different meaning to its modern English usage; it was referring specifically to Gaelic speakers in Britain and Ireland. Only after political changes *c.* 900 is it appropriate to use the term Scots in its more modern sense (see Chapter 7). The names used in this book (see p. 10) are therefore slightly at variance to what most readers may be familiar with, but they reflect better the political circumstances.

## Who were their neighbours?

The Picts and Dál Riata had a number of contemporary neighbours whose interrelated history was instrumental to their mutual development and will be discussed where directly relevant. To the south of the Forth–Clyde isthmus the Romans were familiar with a number of native British tribes: the Votadini, Selgovae, Novantae and Damnonii (see **1a**). These were the people who by the sixth century had evolved into the British kingdoms of Gododdin (from the Votadini) in the Lothian area, Strathclyde and Rheged (in south-west Scotland) (see **1c**). But the Angles – Germanic peoples who first invaded England in the early fifth century – were soon to make their presence felt in the north. Around the mid-sixth century they had established the kingdom of Bernicia in Northumbria, with its stronghold at Bamburgh, and from the seventh century they also gained Lothian (until 973) and, more briefly, territory to the north of the Forth.

Initially hostile to Dál Riata, Picts, Angles and Britons were the Vikings, aggressive invaders from Scandinavia (largely Norway, but latterly Denmark) whose first recorded attack on the British Isles took place in 793 on Lindisfarne in Bernicia. From the following year their attacks increased and were reported by contemporary annals as amounting to 'devastation

rather than Ireland, the member of a new dynasty or simply the first Christian king, and the foundation legend may have been created in response to this.

In most modern literature the Dál Riata are referred to as Scots. This is a direct translation of *Scoti* or *Scotti,* first used by the Classical sources to distinguish them from *Picti,* both of whom are described as early allies in assaults against the Roman empire in Britain. From the mid-fourth century, Britain was being attacked from all sides with the additional aid of the Attacotti (an unknown tribe from either Ireland or the Western Isles), Franks and Saxons. This was part of a European phenomenon of attacks against the empire which culminated, in some areas, in new settlements, of all the islands of Britain by the gentiles'. Shortly afterwards settlers also came. They colonized the northern and western fringes of Scotland, including large parts of both Pictland and Argyll, as well as establishing important bases around the Irish Sea. By the later ninth century a Norse earldom was firmly established in the Northern Isles and Caithness, which owed its allegiance to the Norwegian kings then based near Oslo. Ultimately it was the presence of the Vikings and their continuing expansionist tendencies which were instrumental in the final unification of the Dál Riata and Picts (see **1d**).

## The history of interest in the Picts and Dál Riata

It was primarily the Picts who captured the imagination of early antiquaries and travellers because of their unique symbols and other traditional distinguishing characteristics. This bias in interest continues. Consequently it is not surprising that the Picts are perhaps the most extensively studied and well-flaunted people in north Britain. Research to date on the Dál Riata, while perhaps lesser in scale and certainly less high profile, has none the less the potential to permit a comparison between the two peoples.

Sixteenth-century antiquarians (William Camden or Hector Boece, for example) were interested in the Picts, though their comments are primarily restricted to observations derived from Classical texts. By the eighteenth century, however, travellers (such as Thomas Pennant) and the compilers of the *First Statistical Account* were drawing attention to the existence of surviving physical remains, particularly sculpted stones. It was these carvings which received most attention during the nineteenth century and first half of the twentieth. That their interest extended beyond the stones is confirmed by the publication of more wide-ranging texts, and there was a tendency to ascribe all sorts of monuments to the Picts, particularly brochs ('Pictish towers'; but in fact built by the inhabitants of north and west Scotland from whom the historical Picts were descended). The mid-nineteenth century also witnessed the foundations of serious research into the early historic documentary sources.

But it is only since the 1950s that early historic studies in Scotland fully came into their own, with leaps in our knowledge through excavation, field survey, historical, place-name and art-historical research, enhanced by interpretative analyses of this evidence from a variety of differing perspectives. A major landmark was the Dundee conference in 1952 which culminated in the first comprehensive survey of Pictish archaeology, *The Problem of the Picts*, published in 1955. The memorable title of this volume has unfortunately been something of a hindrance to later studies, since it reinforces the 'enigmatic' aspects of the Picts, and despite the disclosures of modern research it is sometimes still difficult to shatter this perceptual barrier.

But to be fair to its contributors, in 1952 they could not 'point to a single fortress or to a single dwelling or burial and say with certainty that it is Pictish... The problem lies in the recognition or identification of material as Pictish.' This dilemma is perhaps reflected in Isabel Henderson's publication of *The Picts* in 1967. Although the first modern survey, it was heavily biased towards historical and art-historical aspects. Judicious programmes of research and rescue archaeology (in advance of, for example, coastal erosion or quarrying) have subsequently begun to revolutionize our perception of the diverse range of material which survives throughout Argyll, and more particularly Pictland (**4**).

Perhaps some of the greatest advances in Pictish studies has come from the discovery of sites and associated landscapes through aerial photography. Modern land use and soil conditions virtually exclude their discovery in Argyll, however (see Chapter 2). Many of the crop marks are in areas where, in combination

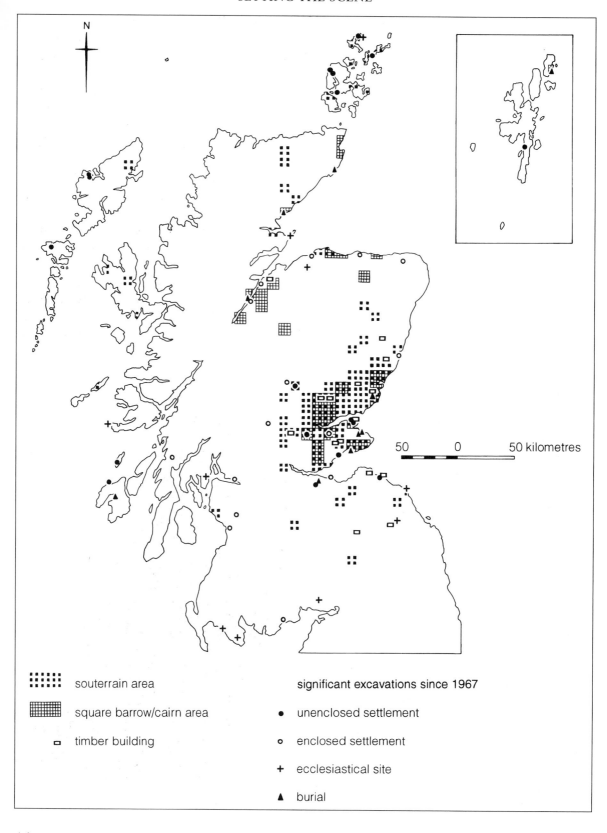

N

50        0        50 kilometres

souterrain area

square barrow/cairn area

timber building

significant excavations since 1967

• unenclosed settlement

○ enclosed settlement

+ ecclesiastical site

▲ burial

4 *Distribution of recent work and discoveries in early historic Scotland. The timber buildings and most of the souterrains (semi-subterranean chambers) and square barrows are known only from aerial photographs.*

with place-name analysis, there is the potential to recognize and understand how early historic landscapes operated. Survey work by the Royal Commission on the Ancient and Historical Monuments of Scotland (RCAHMS), particularly in Argyll and Perthshire, also presents the archaeologist with a virtually untapped source of evidence (both upstanding and ploughed-out monuments). Art-historical research has been prolific, leading to important leaps in our understanding of the development of Insular art and its implications for society as a whole. Published exhibition catalogues and equally lavishly illustrated conference proceedings present a wealth of such data in an accessible form. New historical syntheses have also provided the foundation for future archaeological research. Enough work has been undertaken for us now to step beyond the recitation of catalogues of data and to attempt to understand how society operated. First, however, it is necessary to reconsider some of the myths and legends which cloud modern perceptions of the Picts, and hence create imbalances which complicate interpretations of their relationship with their neighbours.

## How enigmatic are the Picts?

Current learned opinion largely favours Leslie Alcock's view that the Picts were 'a typical north-west European barbarian society with wide connections and parallels' and that they were accepted as such by their neighbours. The major archaeological discoveries since the 1950s and the most recent historical syntheses tend to support this notion.

So why then did the 'enigma' exist? Six key issues can be pinpointed as responsible for the evolution and sustenance of this so-called

'problem': Pictish symbols; Pictish language; matrilineal succession; the 'Foul Hordes Paradigm' (barbarism); the lack of Pictish documentary sources; and the Picts as a lost people. Most of these issues are dealt with in some detail in later chapters. The connecting factor is that they each identified the Picts as being somehow 'different' and cumulatively the impression they built was a strong one.

The Picts would definitely not hold the same place in the hearts of the world if their unique symbols did not exist (5) (Chapter 5). Found in much of Pictland, and almost exclusively there, they comprise a range of diverse motifs which were placed on sculpted stones, cave walls, everyday objects and splendid jewellery. Their precise meaning eludes us, and is likely to remain so, although interpretations abound. But their distinct nature should not obscure the

5 *A Pictish symbol stone at Aberlemno.*

fact that in most other respects the material culture of the Picts was little different from that of their neighbours, with whom they shared much in common. Further, the study of the ornament used in these symbols can contribute to placing Pictish art and society in a wider, more familiar, context.

The notion that some of the Picts, unlike their neighbours, spoke a non-Indo-European language (Chapter 2) is ill-founded. Furthermore, arguments for the unusual practice of matrilineal succession are weak (Chapter 3). (One particularly complicated modern explanation of the Pictish symbols by A. Jackson (1984) attempts to relate all three elements, but it stretches both credulity and comprehension.)

In what has been referred to as the 'Foul Hordes Paradigm' – which comes from a description of the Picts by Gildas, see p. 101 – the Picts were often considered to have been more barbaric and backward than their neighbours. The primitive practice of tattooing their bodies, long neglected by their neighbours, was seen to reinforce this (although its practice cannot be confirmed and the tradition may simply stem from attempts to exaggerate the 'barbaric' qualities of the Picts), while their reputed use of matrilineal succession was said to hark back to earlier times. The aggression and military prowess of the Picts cannot be doubted (as attested in Classical and early historic sources). However, given the warlike nature of society and the wanton aggression of some of its leaders, it is questionable whether they were any worse than their neighbours, who obviously had something to gain in suggesting

how barbaric the Picts were! It was the Romans who had first attempted to conquer northern Scotland, not vice versa. On the contrary, it can be demonstrated that Pictish society was equally as complex and sophisticated as that of its neighbours.

Only one Pictish documentary source survives – the so-called king-lists – and in comparison to contemporary Ireland, Argyll is also poorly served (Chapter 2). This has led to the Picts and Dál Riata being said to lack what has been referred to as 'personality', unlike the 'special character and charm' of their Irish neighbours. The paucity of native Pictish writing has, moreover, given freer reign to more fanciful interpretations of their past.

Finally, early observers perceived the Picts as becoming a 'lost people' shortly after the 'Scottish' takeover (Chapter 7). While some evidence can be brought forward to support this case, it can also be demonstrated that many aspects of Pictish society did in fact continue. However, the 'lost' label has undoubtedly served to reinforce the Picts' enigmatic qualities.

Traditional interpretations are still prone to emphasize the differences rather than similarities between the Picts and the Dál Riata. However, even if non-Indo-European traits did exist, they need not exclude Pictland from the 'Celtic Commonwealth'. Further, there is no suggestion in this book that the Picts were not special, or are unworthy of their modern popularity, but in order to better understand northern British society, it is necessary to look beyond these apparent peculiarities. The discoveries and research since the 1950s present the opportunity to do so.

# CHAPTER TWO

# Communicating with the past: the sources

A wide range of differing sources exists for the study of the Picts, Gaels and their neighbours. While in practice it would be very unusual to use any of these in isolation, each has peculiar characteristics which merit consideration before the evidence presented in later chapters can be interpreted. This applies in particular to the early historic documentary sources.

## Documentary sources

The Picts and Dál Riata lived during the so-called early historic period, known variously throughout the British Isles as the Dark Ages, early Christian period, early medieval period, or Late Iron Age. The term 'early historic' was first coined to emphasize the availability for the first time of local (in the sense of non-Classical) sources.

Although documentary references to the events of the fourth to mid-sixth centuries in Scotland are few, these and later sources have the potential to provide evidence for a general political background against which the archaeological sources can be reviewed, and also evidence for specific events which are unlikely to be recognized on archaeological grounds alone. Most sources tend to only refer to major political events and are not directly concerned with ordinary people. Fortunately the authors sometimes included incidental information about daily life which, although insignificant to them, can be very useful to us. In addition,

external sources (particularly those from Ireland and Wales) provide a basis for interesting yet informed speculation about the nature of both Pictish and Dál Riata society.

However, the value of documentary sources lies not just in the direct archaeological or political implications of their content, but in consideration of the social processes which brought them into being and what lay behind their production and preservation. Any document tells as much about the time it was written as the time it purports to describe. History is always being rewritten by the present generation.

In general terms, a number of factors must be borne in mind when considering how reliable any documentary evidence is. Firstly, who or what were the sources and how reliable can they be expected to be? Did the writer have direct experience of the events being described and how long after the event were they being recorded? This is important to know, since documents may record traditions which were transmitted orally over generations, the circumstances of which inevitably will have led to changes in their content. Secondly, since no original fifth- or sixth-century manuscripts survive, and most are normally copies of copies, what processes have intervened to alter the originals? Scribal error or conscious amendment (perhaps politically motivated) are the obvious problems.

Only one text of any kind can fairly be claimed as Pictish, the so-called king-lists, which give lengths of reigns. The surviving copies fall into two groups, none of which are in a manuscript older than the fourteenth century and one of which is heavily gaelicized. A list compiled in 724 is likely to be derived from annals, perhaps notes kept in the margin of Easter Tables. However, given their late transcription, it is obvious that they contain scribal errors and/or reflect later political interests. The list contains the names of more than sixty kings of whom about thirty may be regarded as historical, in the sense that they are known to us from other sources. The prehistoric part of the list covering the period between about the third and mid-sixth centuries is likely to have been added towards the end of the ninth century. Irish early historic genealogies often claimed descent from a tribal goddess, and the Pictish list might also include figures from mythology, heroic legend and perhaps genealogy, if we were in a position to recognize them. This pseudo-tradition also had political motives (Chapter 7).

Scholars debate whether Pictish scriptoria were ever very active, but the lack of Pictish documents may also be due to the fact that Pictish history and literature were largely oral and vernacular. However, the Pictish kingdom was short-lived and this, in combination with the ravages of time and the fact that documents may have been dispersed in times of social or religious upheaval (such as at the Reformation), should be remembered. The scarcity of sources and imbalance between Dál Riata and Pictish ones, however slight, is unfortunate since this disparity again leads to a tendency for the Picts and Dál Riata to be treated differently both in comparison to each other and in relation to their neighbours.

No separate list of Dál Riata kings pre-dates the eleventh century, but many genealogies are incorporated into the *Senchus fer nAlban* ('History of the men of Scotland'). In its present form, this is a tenth-century edition of a late seventh-century document, and appears to have been written with political motives in mind, since it states that each of the main Dál Riata aristocratic families (referred to as kindreds) was descended from a common ancestor, Fergus Mór mac Eirc. This is likely to incorporate a fair degree of editorial fiction and appears to be a conscious attempt to demonstrate that all Dál Riata owed allegiance to one particular kindred.

Fortunately, references to the activities of the Pictish and Dál Riata royalty and aristocracy are also found in Irish sources which draw on Dál Riata material (none of which now survives in Scotland). Detailed contemporary records of outstanding events were probably being compiled at Iona from the 670s until about 741 and these were subsequently incorporated in Irish texts such as the *Annals of Ulster*. Iona was the pre-eminent monastery in Argyll and mother-church of monasteries on both sides of the Irish sea. As such it was closely involved with the development of the early Church in Ireland; much material (including the *Senchus fer nAlban*) was probably transmitted there due to links between the churches on both sides of the North Channel, particularly when Ionan monks fled to Ireland at times of political pressure and Viking threats. From about 675 to the 740s there may also have been a source at Applecross monastery. The annals (which only survive in later medieval manuscripts, but appear to have been fairly faithfully copied from the originals) therefore provide a good source for events in Argyll and beyond.

The *Old Scottish Chronicle* (preserved in a fourteenth-century manuscript) may originally have been composed in the late tenth century. It is likely to have been partly based on oral traditions and partly on earlier written sources. Probably compiled at the monastery of Brechin, it contains annals and a king-list for the 150-year period following the accession of Cináed mac Ailpín in 842, detailing the infant kingdom's struggle for survival against the Vikings. It is particularly important because it belongs to a period when northern English annals cease to be very informative about their Scottish neighbours.

Relevant narrative accounts take the form of contemporary or near-contemporary attempts to describe the history of Britain. They include references to events in Pictland and Argyll, or near-contemporary saints' *Lives,* but only one surviving example was written in Scotland.

Our study would be severely impoverished were it not for the survival of Adomnán's *Life of Columba.* Columba was the founder and first abbot of the monastery of Iona from after 563 until 597. Adomnán (or Adamnan) was one of his successors (679–704) and his account may therefore be reliable in many respects. Here can be found evidence about people and places as well as religious, social and political practice. But uncritical reliance on this single account undoubtedly skews our perception of this period and the role of Columba in introducing Christianity to Scotland. Other saints are less well known: their lives do not survive; they were not involved with such important secular dynasties as Columba; and the monks of Iona set a highly efficient and successful propaganda machine in place. The writings of clerics are unlikely to be devoid of religious or political bias and saints' *Lives* were generally compiled to promote interest in, or the prominence of, a local saint and his or her relics (for early tourists), and to provide evidence for the rights, rents and dues of the churches and the relationships of authority between churches. Adomnán's account is no exception and inevitably contains some partisan views due to his social standing and his direct involvement in contemporary politics (Chapter 3).

The most useful narrative is that finished in 731 by the monk Bede at the Northumbrian monastery of Jarrow: *Historia Ecclesiastica Gentis Anglorum,* 'Ecclesiastical history of the English people'. Bede did use sources which we know to be unreliable, notably an account by Gildas, a sixth-century monk of either Welsh or Strathclyde origin, entitled 'Concerning the ruin and conquest of the Britons' which cast the Picts as 'foul hordes'. But Bede also relied on witnesses and other 'respected and learned men' who sent him reports and whom he was able to interrogate. One such source was undertaking archival research as far away as Rome! Bede was primarily interested in the English nation, but its history, and particularly that of the Northumbrians, was very much tied in with that of the Dál Riata and Picts. His account therefore contains direct and indirect accounts of events which are fundamental to our understanding of the development of Scotland.

The *Senchus fer nAlban,* of the late seventh century, is a rare survival of an early historic survey (civil, army and navy) and genealogy which cites the military dues owed from various parts of Argyll. It gives an accurate indication not only of the scale and approximate location of settlement, but also the complex and hierarchical manner in which society was organized. It is likely to have been compiled for the purpose of informing an overking or some outside authority how much tribute, among other things, could be expected from this area (Chapter 4).

Although charters were widely prevalent in Anglo-Saxon England, no early charters have survived in Scotland. However, there are a number of sources which help us to understand how rights to land and resources were organized. Adomnán's *Life* suggests that the monks of Iona had rights to a wide range of resources from various places (such as timber for building and ship construction) and these are the sorts of gifts of land and/or privileges which we would expect to have been recorded. The ninth-century Gospel book the *Book of Deer* contains Gaelic notes written in the 1130s to 1150s (6). They describe systems of land tenure in Buchan (but probably more widely applicable) relating back to earlier practice and are hence relevant to us. These notes are part of a 'Celtic' charter tradition found in

*6 The* Book of Deer: *later Gaelic notes, recording title-deeds, have been written into the space around the picture of Abraham. This Gospel book (154mm x 107mm/6in x 4¼in) was produced in a provincial scriptorium in the ninth century by a competent scribe. Yellow and pinky-brown paint have been used (by permission, the Syndics of Cambridge University Library).*

western Britain, the ultimate source for which can be found in the late Roman empire, and may imply that there were charters in Scotland from the seventh century.

Although there is an occasional later reference to the fact that laws were promulgated, Pictland and Argyll, unlike contemporary Ireland and Anglo-Saxon England, are bereft of surviving law tracts (such as the Irish *Crîth Gablach* or Laws of Status, which deal with the duties and privileges of various grades of society). Elsewhere these contain a vast array of invaluable information about the structure of society and more mundane details of everyday life (from a list of household contents to agricultural practices, such as bee-keeping, and the physical appearance of buildings).

The *Gododdin* is an account of the defeat of the Britons (of Lothian) by the Angles at Catraeth (Catterick, Yorkshire), and is a very useful account of the warlike and heroic society which existed in northern Britain at this time (although scholars debate whether it is authentically the work of Aneirin, a famous sixth-century British poet).

## Language and inscriptions

Bede states that the four nations of Britain – the English, British, Irish (Dál Riata) and Picts – each had their own language, 'united in their study of God's truth by the fifth – Latin'. The Celtic language group (a branch of Indo-European languages) can be divided into several types and sub-groups from which modern Celtic languages evolved (7). Of these, Q-Celtic (Gaelic) was spoken by Gaels in both Argyll and Ireland, but there used to be considerable controversy over which language(s) the Picts spoke.

It was first suggested in the late nineteenth century that the Picts spoke or retained a non-Indo-European (or pre-Celtic) element in

*7 Summary of Celtic languages showing the possible derivation of the Pictish language, which is also likely to have incorporated pre-Celtic elements. Q-Celtic used the* qu *or* k *sound, where P-Celtic used the* p *sound.*

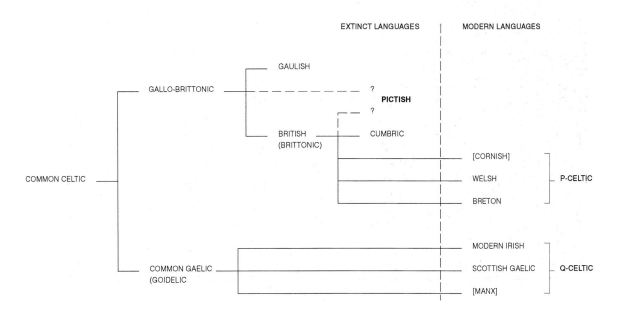

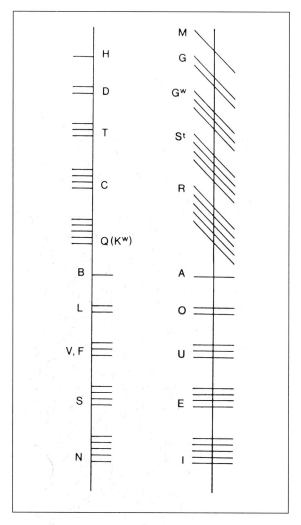

8 *Summary of the main ogham alphabet as used in Scotland; letters are distinguished by strokes on either side of a line and are arranged in consonant and vowel clusters, bearing a resemblance to phonetic principles established by late Roman grammarians.*

Celtic language: P-Celtic. This language, which presumably had many dialects, was different from the Q-Celtic of their Dál Riata neighbours, and this explains why St Columba (a Q-Celtic speaker from Ireland) needed an interpreter to speak to Picts on or near Skye.

Most surviving Scottish early historic inscriptions are in ogham (8), a form of script which originated in a context where Irish was being spoken between the third and fifth centuries. Twenty-nine inscriptions have been found in Pictland, six in Argyll, where they are dated from the sixth to tenth centuries. Katherine Forsyth has now shown (1995) that more texts are comprehensible than previously thought. Many are weathered or fragmentary, but most of those that are still legible record recognizably Celtic personal names. Some are in P- and some in Q-Celtic, reflecting the increasing gaelicization of Scotland. This is important because the decline of the Pictish language is traditionally attributed to the political events of the ninth century (Chapter 7), but this process may have begun far earlier.

Ten inscriptions survive in Pictland that use Roman letters, of which at least seven are in Latin. There are eleven examples from Argyll, of which nine are in Irish. These are usually found in Christian contexts, and imply that a proportion of the population were conversant with Latin. Forsyth has noted that the distribution of these is complementary to ogham, which she suggests was more favoured in secular contexts. A stone from Newton has an ogham inscription down one side, but there are also six lines of an unknown (?debased Roman) script which are indecipherable (9).

Despite their infrequency, the importance of these inscriptions should not be underestimated since they are the only contemporary written native 'records'. Their significance therefore extends beyond what they actually say and the style of the script, to where and on what they are written, by whom and for whom they were created, and how they were actually

their vocabulary. In other words, the language which was spoken by the native inhabitants of the British Isles prior to the movement of Celts (Indo-Europeans) from continental Europe after *c.* 1200 BC. If true, this would have strongly demarcated the Picts from their neighbours and might imply the continuity in Pictland of other unusual practices. However, very recent research suggests convincingly that the Picts spoke only another type of

9 *The Newton stone, from Aberdeenshire, as illustrated by J. Skene in 1832 (RCAHMS).*

10 *'In the name of Jesus Christ, the (a?) Cross of Christ in memory of Reo[...]lius ... on this day'. The longest, comprehensible surviving Latin text, this inscription from Tarbat, Portmahomack, demonstrates that some carved stones were memorials. The style of the lettering suggests the influence of Northumbria and a date in the late eighth century, corresponding with the historical evidence for links between the Pictish and Northumbrian Churches (NMS).*

used (**10**). While inscriptions may do little to augment the historical framework, they do, very importantly, indicate the presence and extent of literacy.

## Archaeological sources

The archaeological evidence for the Picts and Dál Riata consists of surviving physical remains: upstanding field monuments, soil or crop marks, sculpted stones, artefacts and eco-facts (environmental evidence). Inevitably the physical evidence is prone to multiple interpretations, and the resolution of these will hopefully continue to be the subject of healthy intellectual debate for many years to come. But

11 *Newton, Islay: a combination of limited excavation and analogy would suggest that these crop marks are a cemetery of approximately the fourth to eighth centuries. The ditches around ploughed-out barrows (earthen mounds) can be seen in the aerial photograph as dark rings, since deeper soil retains the moisture longer than the surrounding areas (RCAHMS).*

regardless of the approach taken to understanding the evidence (and this book largely presents one set of preferred views), a common problem is the identification of material as relating to either the Picts or Dál Riata in the first place.

Over 80,000 archaeological sites of all periods are recorded in the National Monuments Record of Scotland, and this number rises annually as new sites are discovered. Yet only a very small proportion of these have been, or ever will be, excavated and dated. On the principle of working from the known to the unknown, most monuments therefore need to be interpreted by analogy of their physical characteristics (morphology) with known sites which are considered distinctive enough to be grouped together for purposes of analysis and, hopefully, chronologically specific (11).

But this method is obviously prone to errors, since superficially similar features may not only have different functions but totally different dates. For example, while some rectangular timber halls (recognized only from crop marks; see 4) are known to be early historic in date, one of the few to be excavated (at Balbridie in Deeside) has been demonstrated to be Neolithic, or over 3000 years older than the Picts! Coupled with the enormous potential for regional diversity and the small-scale and geographically biased nature of previous excavation, many subtleties in the record will inevitably pass unnoticed. This applies equally to ploughed-out sites and upstanding monuments. Interpretation of crop marks is often complicated by the fact that they may represent a range of sites the upstanding equivalents of which no longer survive (since they were made of timber), or have not yet been noted. Furthermore, since crop marks can only be recognized in certain types of soil (generally cultivated land, hence usually the better soils of the lowlands) and under favourable climatic conditions, their potential for recovery is geographically predetermined. In addition, since different social and economic circumstances may previously have existed in the lowlands and uplands, we cannot necessarily expect the same range of monuments to have existed in each area in the first place. Crop marks therefore have only the capacity to identify a part of the full archaeological complement and they cannot be positively dated without excavation. Distribution maps of all monument types may therefore be biased for a wide range of reasons.

Although confined to high-status sites, documentary sources can be used to identify monuments which are contenders for early historic date. Fortunately a characteristic feature of the annals is the frequency with which sites in Scotland, largely hilltop fortifications, are mentioned. A successful campaign of trial trenching by Leslie and Elizabeth Alcock has confirmed the identity of some of those sites whose dates and location could be inferred from the sources.

The accurate archaeological dating of sites is largely dependent on evidence from excavation. Hopefully this produces datable material from contexts which can be securely related to identifiable phases in the site development. Alas, much of the material to hand is from earlier excavations, particularly nineteenth-century ones; usually this is poorly (if at all) stratified, and the sequence of events badly understood. Attempts to reanalyse this material and earlier accounts of discoveries, some now lost, has, however, met with limited success; early historic activity can often be recognized, even if its precise nature remains elusive.

Absolute dating techniques are commonly used, principally radiocarbon (C-14) dating, thermoluminescence (TL) and dendrochronology (tree-ring dating). In the early historic period, C-14 and the less commonly applied TL, often with dating brackets of up to several hundred years, do not tend to provide the tightly defined dates which are required to synchronize the archaeological evidence with the emergent political scene. Also, the dating brackets they provide are so wide that it is impossible to correlate observations accurately. Hence short-lived, widespread but specific phenomena, which may be of long-lasting significance, can pass unnoticed. Dendrochronology, on the other hand, has the potential

for accuracy to the calendrical year. But it relies on the survival of assemblages of sufficiently large oak timbers to provide a distinctive sequence of tree-ring widths which can be measured and matched against a dated master chronology. If all the sapwood survives, the exact year in which the tree was felled and, by implication, the related building activity, can be calculated. A calendrically dated chronology covering 7000 years has been constructed using Irish oak, and this has been used to date two early historic chronologies from Buiston and Whithorn, both in southern Scotland. The existence of these chronologies will facilitate the construction and dating of new Scottish material in the future.

Certain years stand out in the tree-ring record as marking periods of extreme environmental hardship (so-called 'marker dates'), when trees put on very limited growth, resulting in narrow tree rings. These correspond to major acidity layers and/or disturbance in Greenland ice-covers and it has proved possible to correlate some of these dates with major volcanic eruptions. The dust veils caused by these eruptions led, it is argued, to substantial environmental changes in those areas where they settled, resulting in declining agricultural yields and impoverished health, often through disease. Without the precision of the dendrochronological dates, these 'specific' events might otherwise have passed unnoticed. Fortunately it is now sometimes possible to recognize layers of tephra (volcanic ash) on archaeological sites, and the recognition and dating of these is an area which is being actively developed in Scotland.

Significant in this context is the fact that one of these marker dates is 536–45, when plague, appalling weather and famine are recorded across Europe (including Ireland). There is as yet no evidence of a major volcanic eruption to account for this, and a large meteoric impact (or a series of impacts) is not out of the question. Sudden changes in the archaeological record at this time have been noted in

Ireland and Germany, and we might anticipate similar abrupt changes in Scotland. However, we must beware the pitfall of assuming that events, imprecisely dated by C-14, can be attributed to the presumed social upheaval following in the wake of these mid-sixth-century natural disasters.

Given the problems with absolute dating in the early historic period, its use is usually regarded as secondary in importance to relative dating methods. These rely on the presence of Roman artefacts, fine metalwork, imported glass, Mediterranean and Gaulish pottery and, as discussed above, documentary sources. But in the absence of a coin-using economy, many of these can only be broadly dated themselves and tend to have limited geographical and chronological applicability. In particular, few artefacts can yet be independently dated from the fourth to seventh centuries. Some artefacts *may* date to this period (bone and antler combs and pins, metal pins and brooches, Class I stones and portable objects decorated with Pictish symbols, parallelopiped dice, painted pebbles and artefacts with ogham inscriptions), but need not do so exclusively. Likewise, some fine metalwork (certain penannular brooch and stick-pin types, as well as more unusual items such as silver tableware, scabbard fittings or reliquaries) may belong to a slightly later period, but these are not only rare, but have scarcely ever been found stratified during the course of excavation (**12**)!

More mundane objects, such as handmade pottery, tend to be produced locally and to have a restricted distribution. Until very recently there was little scientific work on identifying and dating early historic pottery styles, but now distinctive, albeit localized products, have been identified in the northern Hebrides (so-called Hebridean Plain Style) and Orkney.

The extent to which Pictish and Dál Riata material culture can be distinguished is important if the interrelationship between the two is to be fully teased out. However, it is clear that

**12** *The Aldclune brooch: this early ninth-century cast-silver brooch with glass insets was found in Perthshire during the course of an excavation overlying a fortified site, where it may have derived from later settlement, or possibly a burial (NMS).*

a large element of their cultural repertoire seems to be shared between themselves and their neighbours. The Picts' appears to be more distinctive than the Dál Riata in so far as certain types of cultural characteristics have been defined as Pictish by virtue of their date and geographical location. Unfortunately, most of these defining features are absent or not common in the north-west or central Scotland. It is therefore difficult to establish on this basis whether some areas were Dál Riata or Pictish at any one time. There was already a long tradition of a distinction between the west coast and islands from the east side of Scotland. Hence there is no reason to assume that the Picts of north-west Scotland would have been living in the same type of houses or adopting the same practices as Picts many miles away in eastern Scotland. The use of distribution maps, in isolation from an appreciation of the wider context of contemporary society, is obviously prone to misinterpretation.

In Argyll no type site or artefactual assemblage can be identified, leading Leslie Alcock to conclude that 'the *Scotti* came without luggage'. This problem is exacerbated by the fact that we do not know when the Dál Riata first arrived, if indeed the tradition of a mass migration is true. On the basis of the likely dating, provenance and distribution of third-century BC and fourth-century AD Irish and north British metalwork, it has been suggested that two periods of Irish influence and (presumed) settlement can be identified: during the last two centuries BC to the Northern and Western Isles and the extreme south of Scotland; and into lowland Scotland during the first two centuries AD. This argument is based only on a few artefacts, and does not resolve the specific issue of the traditional migration from Antrim to Argyll. But since it is not possible to define any characteristically Irish Dál Riata features (other than perhaps a spiral ring-pin, only two of which ever reached Scotland), then there is little point in expecting to find archaeological evidence for the supposed migration. Indeed, we should question what we might realistically expect to find. Dál Riata material culture shares much in common with that of its Irish Sea neighbours and anyway, if the migration only entailed the small-scale movement of a ruling group, then we need not necessarily expect an influx of specifically Irish material in the first place.

Under these circumstances one has to wonder whether the arrival of the Dál Riata would even have been recognized were it not for the historical and linguistic evidence. Certainly, on the basis of the archaeology alone, it is almost impossible to identify whether sites were either Dál Riata or Pictish, although general diversity can be recognized across Scotland as a whole.

## Art history

Art-historical evidence for the Picts and Dál Riata comprises not so much a different resource, as an application of a different set of skills and approaches to aspects of the archaeological record: specifically decorated objects. Very few upstanding buildings of this period survive, and they lack closely datable architectural details. Style and decoration can provide a framework for dating, while analysis of design, symbolism, form, craftsmanship, function and use have the potential to provide information about the negotiation of social relations: the nature of human contact and communication, religious ideals, political aspirations and cultural contacts. It is at this level that the full potential of art history is realized and its discoveries can be related to historical developments.

Analysis of style and dating have always to be the first step. This is not easy. They rely on the construction of a dating framework which is keyed into 'known' horizons (such as the date of production of a particular manuscript), into which pieces are then fitted by expert consensus. But the experts are not always in agreement about the date and provenance of their points of reference. For example, the animal and abstract-symbol designs of some Pictish carvings belong stylistically with Irish and English metalwork, manuscript decoration and sculpture of the seventh and eighth centuries (13). But not only is the date of some of the manuscripts unresolved, there is also disagreement about which directions influence went in; hence the date of Pictish symbols is also disputed (Chapter 5).

The problem of distinguishing between Picts and Dál Riata is also apparent in their portable artwork, the provenance of much of which is disputed. In this period the art in Ireland and Britain in all media was highly interdependent. This is why the term 'Insular' is used to describe it. The date and place of origin of the *Book of Kells* (**colour plate 1**) has long been disputed: scholars have previously put forward arguments for its production in a scriptorium in Ireland, in Northumbria, or even in eastern Pictland, although Iona is now the preferred choice. The influence of Pictish and Northumbrian art can readily be seen, but this is not surprising since the book was produced during a period when there was plenty of scope for the peaceful integration and sharing of ideas.

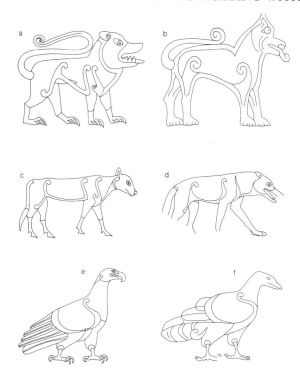

**13** *Comparison of animals in Insular manuscripts and on Pictish carvings:* (a) *lions from the* Book of Durrow *and* (b) *from Papil (in reverse);* (c) *calf from the* Echternach Gospels *and* (d) *wolf from Ardross;* (e) *eagles from the* Corpus Christi College MS 197B *and* (f) *Knowe of Burrian.*

## Place-names

Through analysis of their distribution in time and space, modern place-names can provide a unique insight into the nature of society: the form and organization of settlements; social structure; land use and tenure; and the appearance and ordering of the landscape. The names on modern Ordnance Survey maps need to be stripped back to their earliest meaningful, interpretable and (hopefully) datable forms. This is a difficult task in Scotland where so many languages have been used, sometimes in quick succession, yet much success has been achieved by examining local pronunciations and the early written records. But the earliest dated form of a name (unlikely to pre-date the arrival of Anglo-Norman influence in Scotland in the twelfth century) is only an indication of the time before which it must have been created. Therefore names are also dated by looking at, among other things, their geographical situation or embedded personal names, and how these relate to the known political scene. For example, a Scandinavian name will not be any earlier than the late eighth century, although its inclusion in a place-name need not imply that the creator was actually Scandinavian, or that the place was a part of mainstream Scandinavian settlement.

A range of Pictish, Scandinavian and Gaelic place-name elements have been identified which have a direct bearing on the analysis of Pictish and Dál Riata settlement. Examination of their geographical distribution is most illuminating, albeit problematic, since analysis must consider not only when the names were created but when and why they may (or may not) have ceased to be used (**14**). Since the Pictish language is now recognized as P-Celtic, there is the added difficulty of distinguishing Pictish from its British neighbours.

By far the largest part of Scotland is covered with the early Gaelic names *baile* ('a settlement') and *achadh* (literally 'field', but subsequently applied to settlements). *Baile* is suggested to be an accurate toponymic marker for the area of permanent settlement of Gaelic speakers in Scotland, and includes those Pictish areas which were subsumed after the Dál Riata takeover in the mid-ninth century. Simon Taylor suggests that Pit- and Bal- names were sometimes used interchangeably in the Gaelic-speaking period. Slightly later, *achadh* represents the consolidation of this settlement. Their absence is notable from Orkney, Shetland and east Caithness where Dál Riata settlement did not extend due to the prior presence of the Scandinavians. The situation is slightly different in the Western Isles and Skye, whose people probably originally spoke Pictish

**14** *The approximate distribution of Gaelic, pit- and Scandinavian place-names.*

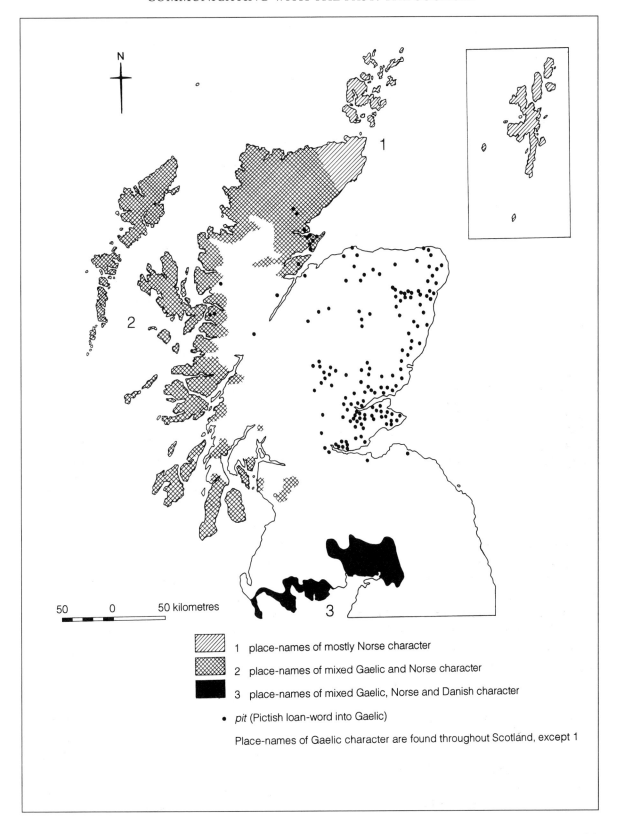

N

50     0     50 kilometres

1   place-names of mostly Norse character

2   place-names of mixed Gaelic and Norse character

3   place-names of mixed Gaelic, Norse and Danish character

•   *pit* (Pictish loan-word into Gaelic)

Place-names of Gaelic character are found throughout Scotland, except 1 and/or Gaelic prior to the arrival of the Vikings, but where these early place-name forms were largely eradicated, or never formed, due to the domination of the Scandinavians and *despite* the ultimate survival of the Gaelic language.

While *baile* and *achadh* may represent the maximum extent of the use of Gaelic, the more limited use of *sliabh* ('mountain', or 'moor-land') and *cill* ('church', indicating the extent of Irish ecclesiastical influence, largely prior to the mid-ninth century) represent earlier phases of Dál Riata expansion. These names also well illustrate the potential of place-names to pro-vide evidence for events which are otherwise unrecognized. Also found in south-west Scotland, it would therefore appear that, at around the same time as the traditional incur-sion of the Dál Riata to Argyll, another movement of people and Irish influence took place there. This event is not recorded in the documentary sources and could not be inferred from the tenuous and limited archaeological evidence alone (although there is slight evi-dence for Irish ecclesiastical influence).

At least seven place-name elements are con-sidered to be Pictish or of Pictish origin: *pett* (with over 300 examples), as in Pitmedden or Pitcaple; *carden* 'thicket'; *pert* 'wood', 'copse'; *lanerc* 'clear space', 'glade'; *caer* 'fort'; *pren* 'tree'; and *aber* 'confluence', 'river-mouth'. Names with *pett* (usually Pit- in modern Scots and English) are not only extensive, but it has been suggested that their distribution is more or less identical to the settlement area of the 'historical Picts'. This is not strictly speaking true, since the place-name element is not found in those areas of former Pictland which were subsequently inhabited by the Scandinavians. This was probably due to the thorough way in which all pre-existing names were eradicated in these areas. And by the time Gaelic (re)-established itself in those areas in the later medieval period, *pett* no longer formed part of the name-giving vocabulary. However, there is no doubt that the word was adopted for a time by the Gaelic-speaking inhabitants of *Alba*, since most of the Pit-names have a Gaelic second element.

The overall distribution of these early his-toric place-names gives a general impression that the settlement (for which place-names sur-vive) was largely confined to better agricultural land. While this may be a true reflection of the majority of settlement, the more inhospitable areas in between were not necessarily uninhab-ited or unused, and would certainly have had strategic significance, not least as routes of communication. So, while accepting that lin-guistic boundaries might not be the same as political boundaries, this does create peculiar problems when trying to identify the cultural affiliation of these intermediate areas, which cover substantial parts of Scotland.

We have now seen why this period can be described as 'early historic'. Data collection still has far to go and each range of evidence has different potential and limitations. But the opportunity exists to piece the evidence together to proffer an overview of how society developed during the years leading up to the birth of *Alba*.

# CHAPTER THREE

# The residence of power

The evolving nature of kingship holds the key to the main historical developments of the early historic period. In Pictland the fifth to ninth centuries witnessed a gradual move away from petty kingdoms to the increasing centralization of authority over far-flung territories, however nominal this might be in practice. This was a process which involved an initial phase of confederation of the various Pictish peoples followed by a long phase of consolidation. The date of inception of this process is very important. These developments are the history of kings and nobles, individuals who acquired and wielded authority by creating and maintaining imbalances in power between people; it is these relations of power which we need to try to elucidate if we are to unravel meaning from the past. Successful leaders are likely to have combined the ability to create wealth with a belief system which sanctioned and legitimized their existence, effective military organization, and the administrative means to control expanding territories. In practice these areas of activity are inextricably entwined and impossible to disentangle, but these different sources of power can be examined: political (below); economic (Chapter 4); ideological (Chapter 5); and military (Chapter 6).

Politics here involves a 'top-down' approach or exploration of the structure and organization of society, particularly the nature of kingship, complemented by the archaeological evidence for power centres. Chapter 4 takes the opposite approach, looking at the organization of the land, the ultimate source of all power, and the ability of potentates to exploit its agricultural potential and control its inhabitants. From this we can begin to piece together a picture of the wider landscape in which society operated and the role which power centres played in controlling and shaping this. Using the top-down approach we can begin to define the levels and scales of society at which we might expect to encounter power centres, suggest the range of likely associated activities, as well as provide a political and ideological framework within which to consider them.

## The structure of society

The early historic period is characterized throughout the British Isles by the emergence of warlike, heroic kings who ruled over defined territories (even though we may not now recognize their precise boundaries). A broadly similar arrangement seems to have developed in both Argyll and Pictland. In part this trend stems from the impact of the Roman withdrawal, and with it the cessation of the formal government and social order with which much of Britain was by then familiar, either directly or indirectly. In the absence of any central authority, local aristocrats began to compete for access to wealth and political prestige, which they could master by access to material resources and the use of violence and personal charisma. Scottish tribes had long since developed into sophisticated social groups which had established a network of contacts with other British tribes during the Roman period, if not before. Although we can question the impact of Roman withdrawal on much of Scotland where Roman direct influence was minimal and/or short-lived, the tribes do appear to have coalesced, at the very least allied to each other during the Roman period, in an attempt to oppose a common enemy. This global alliance may have broken down into smaller groupings once the threat disappeared, and distant intertribal relationships must also have been affected.

Territories began to become more formal because they were the areas within which leaders could protect people and grant them the rights to land. Their (flexible) extent was defined by the radius of a potentate's authority. Hand in hand with the growth of these territories went a fluid transition from a 'tribal' society, where kin-based relations were predominant, to an early 'State' organization, where society was more institutionalized and hierarchical, and relations of clientship became increasingly important. 'Tribal' and 'State' are value-laden terms which mean different things to different people, and in between which (whatever one's definition) are different levels of development and complexity. Without wishing to be too precise (in so far as this is indeed possible) about either Pictish or Dál Riata society, the important fact is that clientship was a means of extending the distance over which relations of authority could successfully operate, and it facilitated the establishment of new elites whose authority might be acquired rather than inherited by right.

At its simplest, clientship (as derived from contemporary Irish laws) generally consisted of the payment of a range of food renders, other tribute and services (labour and military) to a lord in return for land to farm, protection and patronage, a chain of relationships which included all levels of society. At the top of the chain were nobles, clergy and kings, potentates (usually men) who were both socially and geographically mobile; power was exchanged between them either through agreed modes of inheritance and/or aggression. Authority was determined by the number (and type) of clients one could support, which was ultimately dependent on the ability to exploit the agricultural resources of the land. The size of territories expanded when the lord of one area accepted the authority of another; physical conflict was the result when two authorities could not accept who was the stronger, and this appears to have been a frequent occurrence.

But however many levels of lordship existed, the primary economic unit was the individual household or family, and this continued to be the case throughout the period. Contemporary Ireland was divided into *tuatha,* tribes or territories consisting of large groupings of households which were ruled by a king supported by a retinue of specialist staff; kings of individual tribes owed their allegiance to kings of groups of tribes, who in turn owed their allegiance to kings of provinces and, ultimately, to the king of all Ireland. As J. Campbell says, 'this was a world in which there were hierarchies of kings and relativities of kingliness' (1979). With time the geographical extent of kings' authority expanded as power became increasingly centralized. But in the absence of certain resources and technologies there was inevitably a limit to the geographical extent over which authority could effectively operate, as we shall see. Examination of the historical sources provides clues as to the extent of the territories, the nature of kingship and the relationship between kings.

## Territorial divisions

Working back from late ninth-century documentary sources, it appears that there were at least seven provinces in Pictland which may have had a considerable antiquity. The earliest

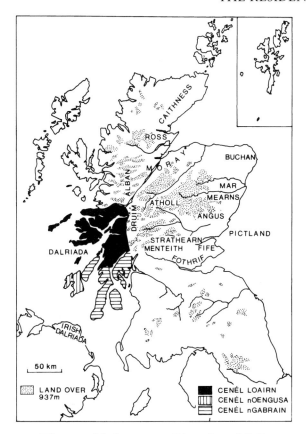

**15** *The possible location of Pictish and Dál Riata (Dalriada) territories. These are not necessarily contemporary and their extent, number and name varied considerably with time. The boundary between Cenél nGabhráin and Cenél Loairn (somewhere in mid-Agyll) is likely to have fluctuated.*

source is a king-list which contains a pseudo-tradition that Cruithne, the eponymous father of the Picts, had seven sons (*Cruithni* is Gaelic for Picts). The names of some of these correspond to Pictish districts (**15**): Fife – *Fib*; Atholl – *Foltlaid*; Fortrenn – *Fortriu*; Caithness and Sutherland – *Cat*; Circinn; Fidach; and Ce. Although this legend was undoubtedly created to imply that Pictland had long been unified (presumably some areas thought otherwise), the seven provinces, probably more, are likely to have existed, although they probably came into existence at different times. Their description includes all the Pictish mainland, but Caithness would have been Norse by the time the tradition

was included in the king-list; Orkney, Shetland and the Western Isles, all excluded from this description, would already have been under Viking domination for some time.

Other historical sources suggest that stable political entities had developed from the Iron Age tribes described by Classical authors, perhaps as early as the middle of the sixth century. Bridei mac Máelchú is described in the late sixth century as *rex potentissimus* (a most powerful, or very powerful, king) and as having held the hostages of a *sub regulus* at his court. These terms obviously imply different levels of kingship, and may mean that Bridei's power extended over northern Pictland, if not beyond. By the end of the seventh century, a Pictish political entity was recognized by neighbouring countries. According to Adomnán and Bede, there may have been a northern and southern province to either side of the Mounth, perhaps reflecting the bipartite division described by the Classical sources. But as with the Classical sources, we do not know how inclusive or exclusive these areas were, in particular whether they included northern Scotland and the Scottish islands. After c. 900 the territorial term *Alba* replaced the people-based term *Pictavia*, and we can first begin to think of Scots in the modern sense of the term.

Irish annals also speak of Dubthalorc (died 782), 'king of the Picts this side of the Mounth', and it has been suggested that there were effectively two tribal confederacies competing for a single overlordship. Certainly southern Pictland appears to have been dominant by the late seventh century and the term 'king of Fortriu' soon became synonymous with the king of all Pictland. The Pictish achievement was that overlordship of such a far-flung collection of people could become a reality (in contrast to Argyll – see below), however nominal that authority might actually be in practice.

The question of what happened to the local kings is answered when we turn to the Pictish provinces (antiquity unknown), where Irish sources refer to a 'king of Atholl' in 739. Tenth-century and later references suggest that at least two levels of royal administration existed in *Alba*, both of which appear to have Pictish origins. At the top of the scale are *mormaer,* in charge of large provinces (later known as earldoms), some of which appear to correspond with Pictish provinces. These men are likely to have been scions of former tribal dynasties which continued to hold sway at the local level despite 'demotion' to territorial lords as part of the process of confederacy; they were local kings in all but name, but their 'kingdoms' were shorn of their autonomous tribal status. Their duties were both military and fiscal, and their posts may have been heritable.

The second level of royal administration consisted of thanages or shires, the surviving distribution of which appears to have complemented that of the later earldoms; in other words there was possibly a distinction between land which a *mormaer* held (by right?) and the royal lands which were managed on the king's behalf by an official. These were administered by a thane who led its people in war, supervised justice and paid its renders and dues to the king or to an earl, having taken his own share. Their role may have been similar to that of the *exactatores*, men who died in battle with King Nechtán in 729, perhaps in the course of attempting to collect dues. The process of Pictish consolidation is acknowledged to have begun with the introduction of the specialist post of thane, which marks a crucial stage in the development of society when, due to the expansion of their territories, kings were no longer considered part of one's extended family, whether real or fictive. The date of the creation of this system as opposed to its terminology – which is late – is therefore very important but unfortunately open to some debate.

At first the Dál Riata straddled both sides of the North Channel, but Scottish influence gradually diminished: after 575 the Irish Dál Riata were formally subject to Irish kingship yet yielded tribute to the Scottish Dál Riata, until 637 when all Scottish claims to this formally were given up. Historical sources suggest that by this time the lands of the Dál Riata extended from the Mull of Kintyre to Ardnamurchan and included the islands of the west coast, Arran and Bute, although Skye and the Western Isles are probably described as Pictish, while to the east 'the mountains of the spine of Britain' (Druim Alban) are the boundary. The Dál Riata initially comprised three chief groups of people or kindreds: the Cenél nOengusa, Cenél Loairn and Cenél nGabhráin (from whom an offshoot - the Cenél Comgaill - appeared in Cowal *c.* 700 to take its place alongside the other three kindreds). Between them there was rivalry but usually only one overlord, traditionally the Cenél nGabhráin although there were periods when two men shared the kingship. The leadership was temporarily challenged by Cenél Loairn a little before 700, but subsequently returned to Cenél nGabhráin who then held it intermittently and precariously, although they also ruled Pictland from 789 to 839. Documentary sources provide further details of political and social structure. Each of the three kindreds consisted of a series of noble families (nine are suggested for Loairn), whose leaders were perhaps the *comites* referred to as being killed during the course of a sea battle between Cenél Loairn and Cenél nGabhráin. By *c.* 700 the three main kindreds had dissolved into at least seven groupings. It therefore seems that Dál Riata kings were, as Lynch says (1992), 'middle-ranking kings of an increasingly fissiparous set of peoples located within a small but difficult territory', although not without the ability to centralize considerable resources (Chapter 4).

## Patterns of inheritance

Understanding how kingship passed between generations has a direct bearing on how control over territories might change and transfer between people of different races. In the case of the Dál Riata, this is understood to have been by tanistry (as in Ireland), where successors were nominated, often in advance of the death of the king, from alternating eligible kin groups. In the case of kings, where intermarriage between dynasties or races was a common political gesture, this meant the continual growth of the kin group from which a successor might be selected and the likely inclusion of 'outsiders'. In addition, reigns tended to be short, a testimony to the violent hazards of kingship. The outcome of this was that sons rarely inherited from their fathers.

The Picts, on the other hand, are thought by some to have followed the practice of succession through the female rather than the male line, in distinction to all their British neighbours. The argument stems from the fact that Bede states that the Picts gave preference to the 'female royal line', supported by a later medieval Irish legend. Protagonists argue that before 780 no Pictish king is known to have been the son of another and that the relationship between a number of seventh-century Pictish, Northumbrian and British kings can be interpreted as evidence for matrilineal succession in Pictland.

Learned opinion is still split. After all, Bede actually states that the Picts would only use this form of succession in *exceptional* circumstances. Since the likely source of his information was Dál Riata, there may have been political reasons for wishing to further this view. No other early historic sources refer to this marriage practice, and Pictish kings are referred to as 'son of' their fathers. It therefore seems far more likely that patrilineal succession – which the evidence fits equally well – was the norm. Finally, given the supposed significance of women in a matrilineal society, it is surprising that documentary and art-historical sources so rarely refer to them, and never in the context of inheritance; when mentioned, they are simply referred to as mothers, wives, daughters and slaves.

The argument for matrilinearity is often justified by the reputed pre-Celtic nature of Pictish society as testified from their language. But, as seen in Chapter 2, this was Celtic. Patterns of succession did change with the accession of Cináed mac Ailpín: although direct patrilineal succession was not immediate, kingship was more tightly confined to the immediate family of his descendants.

## Political context

Picts, Dál Riata, Britons, Angles and eventually the Vikings, all extended their territories within or into northern Britain. In many instances their aim may merely have been the extortion of tribute from subjected peoples outwith their immediate kingdoms, but there were also more permanent shifts in territories. The ebb and flow of their respective successes provides a political framework without which we can not understand how Pictland and Argyll came to be amalgamated

Political links between Picts and Dál Riata possibly began in the late sixth century when a Pictish king called Gartnait may in fact have been a Gael. It certainly appears that the Dál Riata had their eyes on expansion into Pictland from an early date. The main aggressors against the Dál Riata appear to have been the British of Strathclyde who reached the height of their power in the seventh century and, along with the Angles, also regularly competed for Pictish overlordship. From 631 to 653 there appear to have been three Pictish kings of British descent, but from 653 to 685 Pictland was under Anglian domination, primarily through puppet kings. In 672 one of these (Drest) was expelled by the Picts but, in retaliation, the Anglian king Ecgfrith massacred a Pictish army and with it many of the Pictish aristocracy. Bridei mac Bile, a Briton closely related to the Strathclyde kings, stepped into the power vacuum (possibly at the invitation of the Picts) and under his leadership the Angles were routed at the battle of

*Nechtanesmere* (near Dunnichen) in 685. It was only during the eighth century that the Picts seem to have retained their own overlordship (with one possible exception from 750 to 752, when the British king Teudubr may also have been Pictish overlord for the last two years of his life). Óengus mac Fergusa (Óengus son of Fergus; 729–61) ruled Pictland for over thirty years. One of the most powerful and successful Pictish kings, after capturing the stronghold of Dunadd he also appears to have been overlord of Dál Riata. However, Pictish overlordship was only ever short-lived (741–50). Fortriu was invaded in 768 and, between 789 and 839, Pictland was ruled by the Dál Riata.

The ninth century brought profound change. The Dál Riata were under pressure on their west from Viking attacks, and the Picts were also being attacked from the east. A short-lived Dál Riata dynasty had already established itself in Pictland, but its leaders were apparently killed in 839 after a particularly vicious attack – the dynasty of Fortriu was at an end. Cináed mac Ailpín and his descendants exploited the ensuing chaos and disruption to introduce both themselves and a new political structure into Pictland.

## The character of kingship

The changing character of kingship during this period goes some way to explaining how more permanent structures of government came into existence and the role which the introduction of Christianity played in developing this and the nature of society as a whole. Pre-Christian kings were sacral beings who played a unique role in intervening between people and their gods, beliefs which were enshrined in mythology. They were able to do this through the possession of certain magical supernatural powers, but were aided by a retinue (usually male): priests (or druids) with control over natural and extra-natural powers; poets who were responsible, among other things, for the cultivation of genealogy and origin legends; and

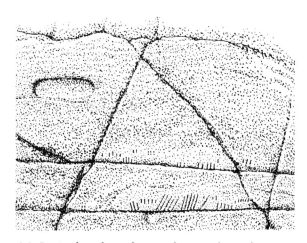

16 *Incised rock surface with one of two footprints and an ogham inscription at Dunadd fort, Argyll (RCAHMS).*

soothsayers who dispensed law. The pagan court of Bridei mac Máelchú, for instance, is described by Adomnán as having included a magician who refused to accept the power of Christianity. Ritual would typically have been associated with the king's role, particularly at inauguration ceremonies. To judge from later Irish sources, these involved a heavy reference to the king's relationship to the gods and his capacity to confer fertility upon the people with whom his greatness was identified.

With one possible exception, no records of Pictish or Dál Riata inauguration ceremonies survive. However, certain sites and features have been associated with them. Carved stone footprints are known to have played a role in ritual from the Iron Age onwards throughout northern Europe, and a number of these have been found throughout Scotland. Several are associated with the entrances to Iron Age settlements in Orkney and Shetland. Examples from Argyll are assumed to have been used in the early historic period, although there is no direct evidence for this. The best-known example comes from within the fort of Dunadd where, by the entrance to the early historic inner citadel, are a series of carvings, specifically two carved feet and a rock-cut bowl (**16**). Given their location immediately outside what had been the Iron Age core of the site, there is a strong possibility that they were carved before the early historic period. However, the addition of an inscribed boar and ogham inscription in the seventh or eighth century suggests that the significance of these features was still recognized then, at a time when northern Britain was Christian. None the less, continued pagan practice is a strong possibility as ritual representations of status do not necessarily change, even under different forms of power. Christian monarchs continued to emphasize their descent from pagan gods and consciously reinforced their position in society by reference to pagan practices, including the selection of sacred hilltops for their power centres. The footprint carvings are permanent features, carved from the living rock, perhaps emphasizing the direct association of a king with the mother earth. The seating of Scottish rulers on the 'Stone of Destiny' at the 'Hill of Faith', Scone is a late survival of this type of fertility rite. As well as being strategically located, these forts were often situated on boundaries where people from different groups could meet to witness the transfer or acceptance of authority between their leaders.

With the advent of Christianity, the nature of kingship was redefined. In theory the Church now interceded on behalf of a king and his people, and clerics began to play a prominent role in inauguration, but in practice some kings acquired saintly attributes and continued to be considered sacred in their own right, in death if not in life. Inauguration ceremonies were of both political and religious significance, since no king succeeded to his throne as a matter of course, and it helped to have the legitimization which the Church could provide. This phenomenon is seen throughout contemporary Europe, but the first recorded Christian ordination of a king reputedly took place in 574 at Iona in Argyll. Adomnán describes how Columba, who had first brought Christianity to Argyll, ordained Áedán mac Gabhráin. There is some debate as to whether this took place. If it did, it may have been a conscious attempt by Áedán to enforce his legitimacy by seeking, through Columba, an alliance with the saint's powerful relatives, the Uí Néill of Ireland. In performing this secular ordination, Columba would have been mirroring the 'divine' ordination which had led to the choice of Áedán rather than his brother as king. However, an alternative view argues convincingly that this event did not take place at all. In 574, although the monastery may incorporate Iron Age earthworks, Iona was a very recent foundation with no tradition of involvement with tribal rituals and hence an unlikely venue for such an event.

Adomnán was a very powerful man, head of the largest monastic confederacy and a member (like Columba before him) of the Uí Néill. As such he had a close involvement in both secular and ecclesiastical politics and his account may be a very clever piece of propaganda. In inventing an inauguration ritual drawn from Old Testament models, Adomnán was the leading advocate of a school of thought which wanted to change the character and succession practices of kingship. Not least he wished to create a more peaceful society in which a king was inviolate, ruled peacefully, and where there was an orderly and legitimate form of succession upon his death (unlike in contemporary society, where succession conflicts often led to bloodshed and feud). The school of thought which he championed was pervasive and influential throughout Europe, as can be seen in the sculpture of Pictland (with its King David iconography; **17**) and Argyll, particularly Iona. A new rite was needed to break with the past but which had its own 'magic', in order to present the new rituals in a traditional manner. Adomnán's aim could therefore have been to make the point that the decision about who ruled the Dál Riata should rest with Iona/the Uí Néill (because Columba had created the precedent) and hence to strengthen the position of the Church in a more peaceful society.

**17** *Cross-slab from Aldbar: King David, accompanied by his harp and shepherd's staff, protects his flock (note the horned sheep) from a lion. Images of David were a popular icon with both religious and secular connotations: God's saving grace and the triumph of good over evil; and the king as a holy warrior.*

**18** *Carved whetstone (140mm/5½in long) from Portsoy, Banffshire (British Museum).*

## Regalia and representations of kings

Certain objects are believed to have been associated with kingly status in both pagan and Christian contexts. In early Welsh literature the ceremonial possessions of a traditional ruler included a sword, knife, drinking horn, cauldron, draughtboard and mantle. In part these relate to other rituals which can be associated with the implementation of royal power: gift giving; feast giving; and hunting and warfare. In Scotland a few objects can possibly be described as marks of office, or even regalia. Secular lords are often depicted on the Pictish carvings with their weapons and sometimes a drinking horn. Little physical evidence survives for these, although the sword chapes and pommels from St Ninian's Isle, Shetland indicate how ornate these could be. There is the possibility that a carved whetstone from Portsoy was an object imbued with symbolic meaning associated with kingship (**18**). A whetstone

19 Carvings of three warriors on a slab from the Brough of Birsay, which also includes carved Pictish symbols (not shown). Note the distinction between the dress, weapons and hairstyle of the man at the front, who is presumably the leader. Such iconography of status is commonly deployed on Pictish sculpture.

20 Map of documented early historic forts and other royal sites in Scotland. A Sites excavated 1974–84 by Alcock and Alcock: 1 Dumbarton; 2 Dunollie; 3 Urquhart; 4 Dundurn; 5 Forteviot; 6 Dunnottar; 7 St Abb's Head; B Other sites with historical references: 8 Dunaverty; 9 Tarbert; 10 Dunadd; 11 Inverness; 12 Dunkeld; 13 Clunie; 14 Scone; 15 Inveralmond; 16 Stirling; 17 Edinburgh; 18 Dunbar.

might be viewed as a phallic symbol related to fertility and it is natural enough to think of it as a symbol of a king's power, the giver and master of the swords of his retinue. In this context it is relevant to note that the whetstone buried in the early seventh-century, rich, royal boat-burial at Sutton Hoo, Suffolk is thought to originate from southern Scotland. Here was a king surrounded in death by objects from all around Britain, Europe and the Mediterranean, a lavish and conspicuous demonstration by his descendants of his power and their reflected glory. The inclusion of a whetstone from Scotland, received from either a British, Dál Riata or Pictish king, was therefore a fitting token of regal respect.

General appearance was also important to status, as so vividly illustrated on the famous carving of three warriors from the Brough of Birsay, Orkney (19). Large brooches appear to have been particularly important (Chapter 4).

## Power centres

Early historic power centres, both secular and ecclesiastical, can be defined as the places where the people who controlled material resources and technologies lived, and from where resources were administered, collected, transformed and exchanged. Inevitably contemporary perceptions of power centres depended on the standpoint of the observer from within the social hierarchy.

Although most power centres are undocumented, some are listed in the surviving documentary sources (which describe the siege, capture, burning or construction of a range of sites) (20). Mere mention will usually imply

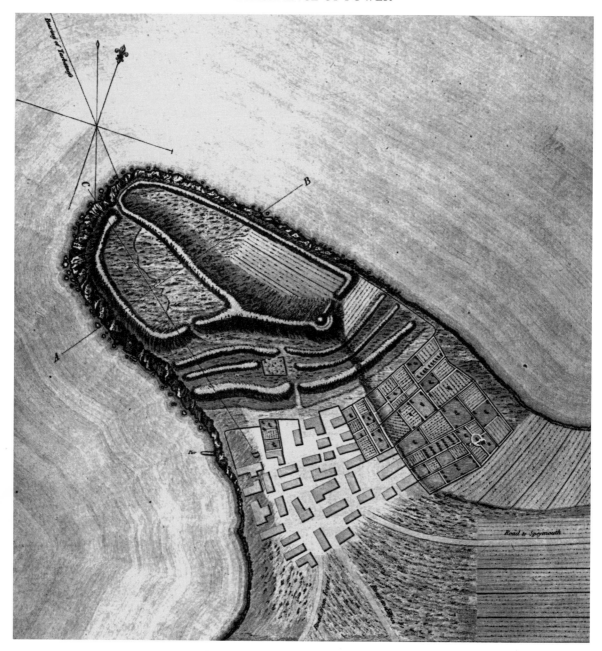

**21** *General Roy's plan of Burghead in the late eighteenth century (RCAHMS).*

that it was significant in the politics of the time and tactical excavation has verified the identification of some of these sites throughout northern Britain. The sites referred to appear to have been local power bases, associated with the leader of one particular group or people competing with another. Whether these are records of the aggressive activities of warrior kings whose aims were booty and tribute rather than the conquest of territory, or scribal shorthand for shifts in the distribution of authority over the areas and peoples associated with these forts is unclear.

The names used for places vary and, while they defy precise interpretation, often appear to imply a political and administrative role in addition to a strongly defended site. In general the named sites are fortified hilltops or coastal promontories enclosed by timber and stone walls and/or timber palisades.

## Forts and coastal promontories

What may be one of the earliest power bases is also the largest (by a factor of three), the coastal promontory fort at Burghead, Moray (**21**). The tip of the long headland is cut off by three lines of earth-and-rubble defences of unknown date, but possibly pre-dating an inner fort, divided into an upper level ('citadel') and annexe, radio-carbon dated to the fourth and sixth centuries. The ramparts of this fort were constructed with a timber framework held together with iron spikes, faced by carefully coursed stone, its interior filled with layers of timber, earth and stone, on top of which may have been a wooden superstructure. Timber-laced construction (sometimes surviving as vitrification) proves to be common to many early historic fortifications, although iron nails are only yet recorded here and at Dundurn. Given its undoubted significance and proximity to an excellent anchorage, it is difficult to avoid the conclusion that this was an important naval base for the Picts from as far back as the late Roman period when Pictish sea-borne attacks are recorded. Nor is there any reason to suppose that the significance of the Pictish navy diminished with time: Bridei 'devastated' the Orkneys in 681, for example. Burghead itself appears to have been occupied until the ninth century, when it may have succumbed to Viking raids. Elsewhere in Moray and Angus, coastal promontories have been demonstrated by excavation to date to the first millennium BC, or more commonly AD, and these were perhaps also 'home ports' for the Pictish navy, although not all were necessarily of high status. Otherwise with the exception of *Dun Fother* (Dunnottar), where excavation failed to locate any evidence for early historic defences, the status of most of these sites is

vague. Coastal promontories are also found throughout the Northern Isles and Caithness, and it is tempting to assume that some of these were not only occupied during the later first millennium AD but were also of high status.

Like most sites north of the Mounth, Burghead does not feature in the surviving annals, but it does share a number of features in common with documented and other likely early historic power centres: its cult and later Christian associations, and the hierarchical use of space.

## Cult and Christian associations

We have already seen in western Scotland how a number of sites appear to be associated with inauguration rituals and belief related to Celtic religious practice (despite the fact that much of this probably took place at natural features, such as groves). In Pictland a number of power centres appear to have either been or have had a close association with religious sites or cult centres, presumably because of the role which kings played in sacred belief and practice. A series of about thirty stone plaques with incised carvings of bulls were originally found in and around the fort at Burghead, of which only six now survive (**22a**). It is not difficult to suggest a connection between these potent symbols of fertility – which were perhaps votive offerings or set in a frieze – with strength and power, the attributes desired by the warlike inhabitants of the fort. Alas, only a small sample of this unique collection now survives, but a single ox-incised plaque was also found on top of the fort at East

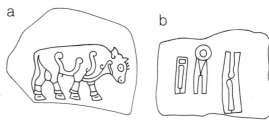

**22** (a) *stone bull plaque (c. 40cm/16in square) from Burghead;* (b) *stone block with Pictish symbols from Gurness.*

Lomond in Fife, suggesting similar beliefs existed in southern Pictland. Pictish symbols, although subsequently adopted by Christians, are likely to have originally related to pre-Christian beliefs, and these have also sometimes been found in contexts which suggest that a ritual or cult focus exists on high-status sites. Most notable is a group of plaques from Dinnacair, a stack site not far from Dunnottar. In this context we should also note the stone with three symbols set into the wall of one of the post-broch buildings at Gurness (see **22b**). Gurness was one of the most important later prehistoric settlements on Orkney and its significance continued into the early historic period.

Further evidence for the likely cult status of Burghead may be seen in the Celtic stone head which reputedly came from the fort's well (**23**). Water gods were important in Celtic religion, and ritual drowning (recalling pagan practice in Gaul) was a traditional means of killing royal prisoners in Pictland, Ireland and, by inference, Argyll. Only 5km (3 miles) away from Burghead, Sculptor's Cave at Covesea

**23** *Sculpted Celtic head found at Burghead. Note the distinctive droopy moustache, hole in the mouth and almond-shaped eyes (Jill Harden).*

contains at least fifteen symbols (probably carved from the fifth to sixth century) and is also likely to have been a ritual site.

We saw earlier how the adoption of Christianity led to the redefinition of kingship and the mutual dependence of the Church and secular authority. Although no churches have yet been found on Pictish or Dál Riata fortified sites, the close relationship between the two powers is expressed in their physical proximity: fragments of a shrine suggest that there was a Christian site immediately outside Burghead fort, while the major monastery of Kinnedar is only about 13km (8 miles) to the east; Mare's Craig adjacent to Clatchard Craig, Fife, produced evidence for burial in long cists and a bell of seventh- to ninth-century date; there is a sub-circular cemetery with an early carved stone at the foot of Dundurn which must surely have an early Christian origin; and Dunadd is within a few miles of Kilmartin church where sculpted stones again suggest an early foundation.

## Hierarchical use of space

Analysis of the architecture of settlements, and their setting, can often provide valuable insights into the development of society, since architecture was commonly the place where most human activity and social interaction took place. Hierarchically organized fortifications have been recognized as a characteristic feature of Scottish early historic forts as far north as Inverness and as far west as Argyll (and further afield), although the scale and physical manifestation of these sites may vary (**24**). Originally thought to have been constructed as unitary monuments, it is now recognized that although they operated as such their form represents the culmination of centuries of development. Understanding when this began, and when the forts reached their final form, is therefore significant if we are to learn how territories formed and power became increasingly centralized. While Burghead may have its origins in the fourth

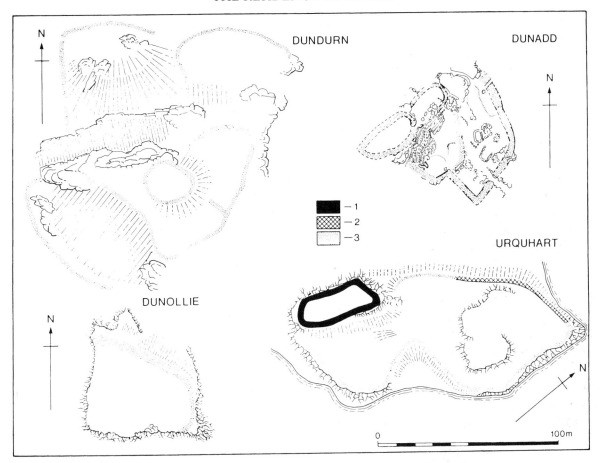

24 Plans of early historic forts (Leslie and Elizabeth Alcock; Society of Antiquaries of Scotland).

century, all other dated forts commence in either the fifth, or more usually sixth, century, and had only achieved their full hierarchical appearance by the seventh or eighth century. Hills with natural terraces were ingeniously exploited by the erection of a 'citadel' on the highest point, with subsequent enclosures usually attached to it. Dundurn and Dunadd are classic examples of this type of development. At Dundurn (colour plate 2) the upper terrace was first enclosed during the late sixth/early seventh century by a stout timber stockade, the living rock having first been grooved in places to receive the timbers. After dismantling, this was replaced by a timber framework (secured by nails) infilled with timber, earth and stone; the recorded siege of 683 may well be the event which led to its destruction by fire. After this, new defences were laid around both the summit and terrace, incorporating masonry robbed from a Roman site about 15km (9 miles) away. The later phases at both Clatchard Craig and the native fort at Inchtuthil also incorporate Roman masonry. We might consider whether stone was now considered more sophisticated, due to its associations with an imperial past. Or did leaders only now have the surplus resources and technology to expend in the transport of these stones, as a demonstration of their wealth and authority? The close-set nature of the outer multiple ramparts at Clatchard Craig is similar to Burghead, but few potential early historic sites with this feature have been excavated, and it is difficult to distinguish these sites from their Iron Age predecessors, especially where hierarchical use of space is absent.

*25  Reconstruction of Dunadd fort, Argyll.*

Early historic forts which developed from scratch in this period also include Dunollie, Argyll, and the British site of *Al Cluith* (Dumbarton Rock, documented between the mid-fifth century and late ninth). But some forts exploited later prehistoric fortifications, either by refurbishing them (as at Craig Phádraig) or by the addition of an internal enclosure to a larger, later prehistoric site to create hierarchical use of space. It matters little whether earlier defences were maintained, since their sheer presence would have created the required depth of space. The hierarchy of the space within the site emphasized the status of its inhabitants (in Ireland status was in part dependent on and dictated by the number of defences one could put around one's site), making its appearance more impressive, creating more controls on access through it, and structuring the activities of the people who lived within it. The nature of approaches and the monumentality of entrances were also important, such as at Dunadd (**25**).

## Use of Roman sites

Unlike Birdoswald, a Roman fort on Hadrian's Wall occupied by a British potentate in the post-Roman period, there is no direct evidence for the continued settlement of Roman fortifications in Scotland. In general the Roman forts were probably too large for early historic leaders to defend, and lacked an elevated situation. One possible exception is *Rathinveramon*, where two ninth- and tenth-century kings died. The rare use of the term *rath* implies an earth bank and ditch, in which case the Roman fort at Bertha, at the mouth of the River Almond and adjacent to the site of the presumed Roman bridge across the Tay, may be a likely candidate, although there are no visible remains. Given the late reference to the site, it may have more in common with the unfortified site at Forteviot than earlier defensive sites, and may only have been sited adjacent to the fort. A number of Pictish power centres are juxtaposed with Roman sites since both were carefully located at nodal points along communication routes – note the apparent concentration of power centres in the area near Perth (Scone and *Rathinveramon*, perhaps the same as *Cinnbealathoir*) – and Roman roads surely survived in use during this period.

We cannot rule out the possibility that some native sites exploited the physical presence of the upstanding Roman earthworks. The clearest suggestions of this emerge at Inchtuthil (**26**) where at one end of the axis of extensive

**26** *General Roy's plan of the Roman and native fort (above 'New Inch Stuthil') at Inchtuthil, Perthshire, in the late eighteenth century. The post-Roman, circular burial monuments are at 'Womens Knowe' (RCAHMS).*

27 *Reconstruction of a crannog.*

Roman remains is a native fort, while at the opposite end are burial monuments, assumed to be broadly contemporary: the Roman remains have apparently created an arena for the conscious exhibition of status and authority at a local power centre.

## Internal buildings

Within these sites we would expect to find buildings fulfilling a wide range of purposes but specifically buildings associated with royal and noble functions, notably feasting. Although Adomnán is not known to have visited Bridei's *munitio* ('fortress'; possibly to be identified with Castle Hill, Inverness), he suggests that it would have included a king's hall (*aula regia*) and house (*domus*). We might also expect to find storerooms and perhaps a treasury, in addition to the full range of domestic and industrial buildings. Unfortunately physical evidence for buildings within forts is elusive, in part due to the lack of investigation of interiors as opposed to defences, but also due to the slight nature of the surviving remains. Many types of timber building (which we know to have been constructed from both archaeological and documentary sources), particularly those constructed from a wooden beam laid directly on the ground, would not necessarily have left much evidence for their existence. Adomnán describes the collecting of rods for

wattling and dressed oak and pine over considerable distances. There was a wattle floor at Dundurn and also limited evidence for wattle and daub.

## Crannogs

However, not all power centres were fortified, although natural features might be exploited to afford some protection. Some crannogs or 'built-up' islets (**27**) may have been high-status sites, as in southern Scotland (Buiston, Barean Loch and Milton Loch), Ireland and, in one instance, Wales. Without excavation it is impossible to either date or identify the status of a crannog. So while they abound in much of Scotland none has yet been identified as Pictish and only Loch Glashan has produced evidence of early historic occupation in Argyll. This dates from the seventh to eighth centuries, and the presence of metalworking, imported pottery and an ornate penannular brooch indicate that its inhabitants were of high status, possibly royal. Other crannogs may simply have been the defensive farmsteads of single families.

## Unenclosed sites

Although enigmatic, Forteviot (*Fothiurtabaicht*) in Strathearn probably provides us with the best indications of what an early historic palace (*palacium*) consisted. In terms of its components, it would have been on a par with a contemporary Carolingian palace. Although not the only palace referred to, it is the only one whose location has been identified with any certainty. Tradition and other sources refer to its existence as a royal site for the late 'Pictish' kings (the last of whom was slain there) and during the early years of the amalgamated kingdom. Later medieval sources imply that it was still considered a royal site in the twelfth century. The inferred existence of a late ninth-century royal chapel (**28**) and the presence of an extensive crop-mark complex

**28** *Forteviot arch, recovered from the Water of May beneath 'Haly Hill', and presumed to have been part of an ornate chapel (NMS).*

noted since 1975 (including early historic burials) add weight to the suggestion that the palace was near here (**colour plate 3**). The actual palace site has not been identified and, like the chapel, it may have been swept into the river. No traces of an enclosure survive in the vicinity and, by analogy with the Bernician royal sites of Yeavering and Milfield, or the presumed Anglian settlement at Sprouston, it is assumed this complex would not have been heavily fortified. However, a palisaded enclosure, if it existed, could have constituted a significant physical barrier.

The Pictish royal centre at Scone (the *Caislen Credi* of 728), which Cináed mac Ailpín deliberately cultivated to become a holy royal centre and inauguration site (perhaps bringing to it the Stone of Destiny), may have been a similar type of site to Forteviot. But with the exception of Moot Hill (the 'Hill of Faith') no upstanding remains have survived the construction of the later medieval Augustinian abbey.

The Brough of Birsay might also be described as an unfortified site, although it is on a tidal island (there is debate as to whether this was the case in the early historic period). This appears to have been the most important early historic site in the Orkneys, an assumption largely based on its finds, location and subsequent importance in the Norse period. The site produced a large number of Pictish pins and combs associated with debris for the manufacture of fine metalwork in the late eighth century. In addition there is a fine slab decorated with figures of Pictish warriors and symbols (see **19**). The lack of farming-land on the island clinches the argument for it being an important secular site dependent on resources from the mainland. Seventh/eighth-century Pictish structures have been identified in excavations, but there is insufficient evidence to suggest what the overall layout of the site might have been.

## Association with prehistoric ritual landscapes

One important feature which Forteviot shares in common with many other early historic

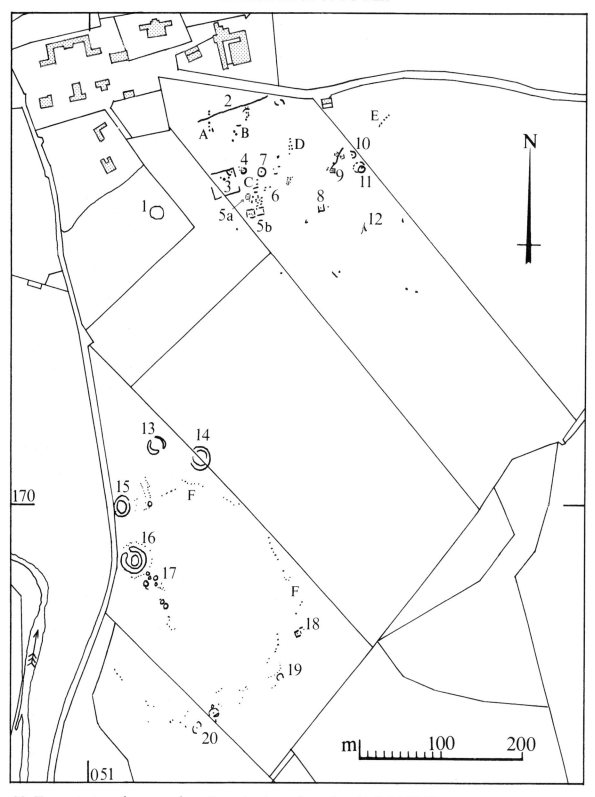

**29** *Transcription of crop marks at Forteviot (see* **colour plate** 3*) (RCAHMS).*

royal sites throughout northern Britain and Ireland, is its association with a major prehistoric ritual complex, as revealed by aerial photography (**29**). It is likely that many of these features, notably the late Neolithic henges (**29**: 13, 16), were still upstanding. The apparent siting of burials (**29**: 18, 20) around the edge of an enormous palisaded enclosure (**29**: F) also suggests that earthworks associated with this were still visible. There can be no question of direct continuity of function, but the social elites may have deliberately used or associated themselves with these monuments of the past in order to both promote and legitimize their own interests. At a more prosaic level, the henges might even have formed arenas for public assemblies and courts, which were usually held in the open (only Yeavering in Northumberland is known to have had a specially designed open-air theatre). Dunadd, sited at one end of the Kilmartin valley, in an area best known for its ritual and ceremonial importance in the Neolithic and Bronze Age, is another such example, with the early Christian focus at Kilmartin, probably a monastery, at the opposite end. The dedication at Kilmartin to St Martin may also be significant, since his cult was popular in the early Irish Church and was associated with the conversion of important pagan sites. There remains the exciting possibility that a contemporary landscape may lie sealed beneath Crinan Moss, the peat which apparently began forming around Dunadd in about the tenth century.

## Hierarchy of power centres

Given that the upper echelons of both Pictish and Dál Riata society consisted of different levels of kings and nobles, we might anticipate that a distinction would be apparent between their sites, although any such distinction is scarcely marked in the documentary sources. The concept of a chief place appears to have existed, since Adomnán refers to the *caput regionis* ('main place of the area') where

Columba met sailors from Gaul, possibly either Dunollie or, more likely, Dunadd. But these cannot be understood as capitals in the modern sense, as places where people also lived who were not directly concerned with government or the royal court and whose main occupation was not agriculture. On the basis of Northumbrian documentary sources there appears to be a threefold hierarchy of royal sites: *civitas*, the principal place in a kingdom; *castellum* or *urbs*, a lesser fortified site; *villa regis*, an undefended palace, residence, township or estate centre. At each of these we might expect to find an assembly place. Alas, there is no easy equation between the suggested social hierarchy, the site hierarchy suggested on the basis of documentary sources and the archaeological field remains, since when excavated these sites often produce the same range of high-status objects. Nor can sites, with notable exceptions, be matched to the historically attested territories which are believed to have existed.

## The changing nature of power centres

The development of power centres parallels the non-static nature of society, which underwent profound changes during this period. The strategic siting of many of the early historic fortifications, such as Dunnottar at the point where the Grampian mountains most closely approach the sea, and their fifth/sixth-century origins, reflect the increasing dominance of new elites whose authority was acquiring territorial definition. As their power increased during the seventh or eighth century they were able to command more resources, both in terms of people and of materials, a substantial amount of which was invested in the creation of larger and more complex power bases where a wide range of specialized activities was under their immediate control. But the authority of the new leaders was constantly contested, as documentary sources intimate, and the kings had to go to enormous efforts to make their physical presence felt throughout the land. By the ninth century many of the earlier power centres became redundant (there is certainly no evidence of activity after about the eleventh century), perhaps as the result of Viking attacks, or their inability to fulfil the requirements of contemporary leaders, and the eastward shift of power from Argyll to Pictland. Power bases moved down from the fortified hilltops to the valley bottoms. This transition must also reflect a growing security and political stability, perhaps fostered by the Church, with which these later settlements may have had a closer association.

We are now at the point where we know what a power centre might look like. But how did it function, what activities were taking place there and what was its relationship to the countryside and its inhabitants? Power stemmed ultimately from the agricultural products of the land, and it is to this which we must now turn.

# CHAPTER FOUR

# Agriculture, industry and trade: the currency of authority

Power came from the land; early historic lords derived authority through their ability to exploit its agricultural potential and control its inhabitants, most of whom would have been involved in producing food. So, by examining the available evidence from the 'bottom-up', we can begin to piece together a picture of the wider landscape in which society operated and to understand better the role which the power centres played in controlling this. But it has to be acknowledged that this is difficult, since documentary sources rarely describe or refer to the activities of ordinary people, particularly women or children, and surviving upstanding field remains tend to be the monumental sites associated with the elite.

## Rearing of animals

Since Neolithic times, people have been farming Scotland from semi-permanent/permanent settlements, developing and refining a mixed economy based on the exploitation of arable, pasture and, where relevant, coastal resources. Annual cycles of production and consumption dominated most of their activities. In early historic Ireland the whole economy revolved around cattle. They were both a measure of one's status and the main source of wealth; lords gave their clients cattle and land in return for food renders, service and surplus beasts. So the number of clients a lord could possess depended ultimately on how many cattle he

could provide. Analysis of the Irish sources and bone assemblages demonstrates that a developed economy existed for the production of dairy products rather than beef (this can be recognized on the basis of the patterns of age at death and sex of cattle).

Evidence for a similar reliance on a dairy economy has been sought in Argyll and Pictland, but as yet there are too few large assemblages from which to confirm this. However, the *Life of Columba* does emphasize the value attached to cattle, with its descriptions of Columba's ability to increase people's fortunes by causing their cattle to multiply, and of the troubles which will befall those who damage them. Later medieval sources confirm the importance attributed to cattle in Scotland, including inauguration rituals whereby new kings carried out cattle raids on their neighbours. Analysis of bone assemblages is always fraught with difficulties, being dependent not only on what part and portion of a site is excavated, but how and where the animals were killed, butchered, cooked, disposed of, and what has happened to the deposits since. The largest relevant Scottish assemblages come from the Northern Isles, where bone tends to be well preserved due to the soil conditions. At none of these Scottish sites have we been able to construct as detailed a picture as we might like, but the potential surely exists. At the fifth- to seventh-century so-called 'princely' site of Dinas Powys in Wales, for example, it could be demonstrated that its inhabitants were not directly involved in dairying themselves (since these had no calves), but were acquiring through exchange the older dairy cows for their meat and hides; a degree of labour specialization and localized settlement hierarchy was deduced from this.

Cattle bones tend to predominate in Scottish assemblages (at c. 50–60 per cent) and in some cases beef is likely to have formed over 95 per cent of meat consumed at any one site. At Buckquoy, a small Pictish farmstead in Orkney (30), about one-third of all animals were killed during their first year for meat and hide, but the majority were kept for milk and perhaps draught. In general the most was got out of animals before they were slaughtered, although calves' hides were valued for vellum and the production of fine leather shoes and garments. At the high-status settlement on the Brough of Birsay, cattle bones predominated but the animals are unlikely to have been permanently reared on the island because there is insufficient pasture; the meat could have been transported over in semi-butchered form, perhaps from a nearby home farm (Buckquoy is an obvious contender) or as part of food renders from clients. Sheep/goat (they are difficult to distinguish) and pig (traditionally associated with Celtic peoples) tend to make up the remainder of most bone assemblages; at Upper

Scalloway (Shetland) pigs became the most important species. At Dundurn and Dunollie sheep appear to have been kept for their meat rather than wool (unlike in Ireland). A similar argument is put forward for Buckquoy, where the sheep may not even have been wool-bearing. Ironically, the opposite is proposed for the Brough of Birsay and this, if anything, emphasizes the difficulties of interpreting bone assemblages. Wool and textile production were perhaps largely confined to lower-status sites, few of which have yet been excavated; spindle-whorls, used for spinning, have only been found on a small number of early historic sites although artefacts associated with textile preparation, notably combs possibly used for carding, are very common on Iron Age sites in the north of Scotland. Textiles produced on the farms may have been brought to the power centres to be exchanged for high-status goods and/or as dues (31).

Coastal resources were immensely important. Fishing extended into deep-sea waters (probably using limpets for bait) and, as well as fowling (including puffins), bird eggs were eaten. Seal meat was also consumed: the monks of Iona had special rights to hunting grounds off Mull.

30 *Reconstruction of Buckquoy, Orkney, with Brough of Birsay in the background.*

**31** *Woollen hood, found in a bog in St Andrew's Parish, Orkney in 1867 and C-14 dated to between* AD *250 and 615. Surviving early historic textiles are exceedingly rare. This was woven on an upright loom and is fringed with a tablet-woven band and long tassels (NMS).*

**32** *Kirriemuir horsemen: note also the well-detailed clothing (Tom Gray).*

Where deer were available these were hunted both for sport and meat; in the Western Isles they appear to have been a staple part of the diet. Horses too were sometimes eaten at the end of their working lives (as at Iona where their hides were also used in leatherworking), but their prime function was in transport, traction and warfare. The prevalence of Iron Age harness pieces in Scotland, and the tribal name *Epidii* ('horses') for Kintyre, emphasizes their importance to the native population for whom they were a symbol of wealth; witness also their frequent portrayal on the Pictish sculpture where their accurate depiction suggests careful selection for breeding (**32**).

## Cultivation

In his *Life*, Adomnán describes the monks of Iona as being involved in both arable and pastoral farming, and the archaeological evidence supports a mixed economy. The arable land would have relied on the dung of the animals and/or seaweed for its continuing fertility.

Surviving plant remains from early historic sites are still few, but different types of wheat, barley, oat and rye are known to have been grown. Flax seeds have also been recognized, in contexts dating from as early as about 5000 years ago, and may have been used for food, oil or textiles, but current evidence for its intensive cultivation begins only with the Norse. Although Adomnán probably refers to a corn-drying kiln at Iona, no physical evidence has yet been found for them; barley was simply roasted above firepits at Dalladies. Rotary querns, however, are a common find on most sites and suggest the widespread processing of grain; the large number from Dunadd suggests centralized agricultural processing for a substantial population. Despite the discovery of a likely millstone on Iona, early horizontal timber water-mills have yet to be positively identified in Scotland, whereas in Ireland they date from the seventh century. It is reasonable to assume that early forms of brassicas – kale, cabbage, turnip and a type of spinach – as well as legumes (peas and beans), were also being cultivated.

Although place-names in *card(d)en* or *pres* ('thicket' or 'covert') imply that parts of Pictland may have been wooded, the distribution of souterrains also suggests that large tracts of the country were being cultivated from the late first millennium BC, if not before. Souterrains are semi-subterranean chambers found throughout Scotland, but particularly Angus and Perthshire, Aberdeenshire, around the Moray Firth, Caithness, Sutherland, and the Northern and Western Isles (see **4**). Most lie in areas of first-class agricultural land (although this may also be due to the potential of these soils to produce crop marks which lead to their recognition). Not only do they come in a variety of shapes and sizes, but their widespread dating implies different functions. The northern examples are earlier Iron Age in date, while the Angus and Perthshire examples (which form a distinctive group) fell out of use in the second or third century AD, when many were deliberately backfilled. The latter group is best understood since most excavation has taken place here and aerial reconnaissance by the RCAHMS has led to a substantial increase in their numbers. Here the souterrains comprise a curving passage (up to 58m long, c. 2.1m wide and 1.8m high; 190 by c. 7 by 6ft) cut into the ground and lined with either stone or timber and wattle, roofed with either stone or timber lintels. There is usually a main entrance at one end, with subsidiary small entrances and/or chambers, although material may possibly have been taken in through the temporary dismantlement of a timber roof. With their year-round, even temperature they are best understood as places for storage of crops and perhaps dairy produce. They indicate that the ancestors of the Picts were well capable of producing, storing and presumably redistributing large quantities of cereal. The long-held suggestion that they were underground byres ought to be dismissed. Because of their ubiquity they cannot be taken as indicators of high status, although the ability to store food would have increased the power and stability of the associated community.

It used to be thought that souterrains existed in isolation but it is now recognized from the evidence of crop marks and excavation that they are usually, if not always, associated with either timber roundhouses and/or stone buildings from which they are often entered (**33**).

As yet the deliberate infilling of the souterrains cannot be satisfactorily explained; the most prevalent suggestion relates this to the withdrawal of the Romans and the collapse of the economies which their presence had created. However, we have seen that the origin of souterrains pre-dates the Romans. Furthermore a similar transformation of settlement forms with pre-Roman pedigrees takes place at roughly the same time throughout Scotland (see below). An alternative explanation is therefore likely.

Settlement did not cease on souterrain sites. There is always a dating problem due to the virtual absence of diagnostic artefacts, but at

Ardestie and Carlungie oval stone buildings overlie earlier features, while at Dalladies a C-14 date from a nearby pit suggests activity in the sixth century. Some of the numerous crop-mark roundhouses, apparently without souterrains, may belong to this later period, as demonstrated by excavations at Easter Kinnear, Fife (**colour plate 4**). These appeared as annular, crescentic or round features, which suggested that at least part of their floor was semi-subterranean. Now confirmed, it is still unclear how these structures worked because evidence for timber construction is lacking; was there a wooden floor over a cellar? Importantly, storage facilities continued to exist. Additionally they may have taken the form of above-ground features which leave little archaeological trace (Adomnán describes several barns at Iona, for example).

If we are correct in assuming that these nucleated settlements are indicative of the extent of agricultural exploitation in Pictland south of the Mounth, then we can understand why this part of Pictland would have been so attractive to outsiders. It also had the potential for the development of political complexity, given its capacity for the accumulation and redistribution of agricultural wealth.

## Other foods

Fungi, wild fruit, nuts, berries and leafy plants were also seasonally available: hazelnuts, raspberries, blackberries, crab-apples, sloes, damsons, elderberries, wild cherries, crowberries, sorrel and docks. A wide range of wild plants - such as scurvy-grass - may also have been used as dietary supplements. Potential flavourings included coriander and dill (recognized at Buiston crannog) and bog-myrtle (which could be used in ale). At Dundurn, much to the surprise of the excavator, the lower levels of the citadel were waterlogged and from among the preserved organic material was recovered human faeces containing over twenty-four cherry stones! This midden also continued a mass of bracken, moss and woodchippings, which had probably been cleared from a building where they acted as flooring or bedding. Bee-keeping is known to have been practised in Iron Age England and honey would have been highly prized as a natural sweetener and as the basis for mead, an alcoholic drink much quoted in the *Gododdin*. Beeswax was also a useful sealant.

*33 Reconstruction of house and souterrain at Newmills. Perthshire.*

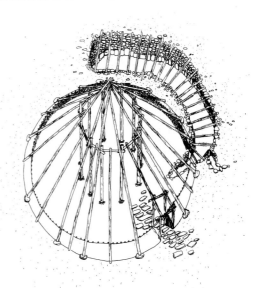

## Fields and trackways

We should therefore expect the countryside to have been a busy, well-managed landscape with fields and trackways (perhaps defined by hedges, hurdles or dykes to protect crops from animals) interspersed with grazing and woodland, some of which was being managed as part of a long-term strategy to produce wattle, charcoal and bark for tannin. At Lairg, Sutherland, in an area which is likely to have only been used for rough grazings over the last 1000 years, rig-and-furrow, field banks and clearance cairns have been found sealed under peat dating to the first millennium AD. If it can be argued that the peat only grew when the cultivation had ceased, then these are early historic fields, which are otherwise difficult to recognize.

## Other settlement types

Even though most people shared the common pursuits of farming and relied almost exclusively on local produce and goods, their farmsteads vary enormously over the country as a whole. Stone-and-timber, oval or round-houses (often with a subterranean component) appear to have been the norm on the lower, more fertile ground of southern Pictland. On higher ground at Carn Dubh above Pitlochry, in an area long used for rough grazing, prehistoric roundhouses were replaced by sub-rectangular structures, possibly from the mid-first millennium, and the burnt remains of a sub-rectangular building dating to the late sixth/early seventh century have been found at Easter Kinnear. Survey in Perthshire led to the discovery of a previously unrecognized series of buildings for which the term 'Pitcarmick-type buildings' has been coined (after the type site) (34). They consist of long houses with a 'residential' area and a larger area with a central soakaway. The preliminary results of excavations by John Barrett and Jane Downes suggest that they belong to the mid- to late

first millennium. The Pictish heartland north of the Mounth has not been so intensively investigated, but there is crop-mark evidence for souterrains and settlement similar to that in the south. Some of the presumed timber sub-rectangular houses found on the east coast may also be early historic in date by analogy with Anglian examples found as far north as Fife (35; see 4).

The dating of Argyll duns poses interesting questions. Broadly speaking they can be defined as thick, stone-walled enclosures, usually sub-circular in plan, varying in size from an internal area of 20 to 375m (66 to 1230ft) squared. At least two-thirds of them are likely to have been roofed over and they can be interpreted as defensive farmsteads. They need to be understood in the wider context of related architecture that is found in the Pictish periphery of the Western and Northern Isles and the northernmost part of mainland Scotland. Here duns and brochs comprise a common tradition of what has been usefully termed 'Atlantic

**34** *Pitcarmick, buildings and enclosure (RCAHMS).*

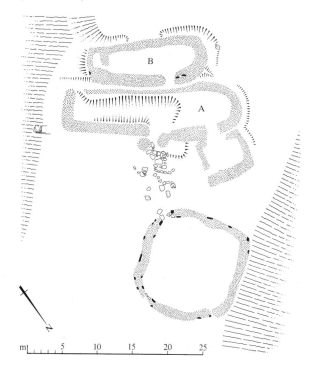

35 *Timber hall in a circular enclosure at Monboddo, Kincardineshire (Ian Shepherd, Grampian Regional Council).*

roundhouses' – monumental stone-built houses some of which have architectural details such as intramural cells or galleries ('complex Atlantic roundhouses') or upper galleries ('broch towers'). It is now considered that these were built between the mid-first millennium BC and the first, if not second, century AD.

In Chapter 3 we saw how some duns appear to have been built in the mid-first millennium AD, if not later. Further east a group of so-called 'ring-forts' found mainly in Strathtummel and Strathtay (Perthshire) is poorly understood. Litigan, the only dated Scottish ring-fort, has produced a C-14 date between the late eighth century to early thirteenth and comparisons have also been drawn with Irish ring-forts which date from the sixth to eleventh centuries.

At some point from the second to fourth centuries most of the Atlantic roundhouses cease to be occupied in their original form. Excavation since the 1970s at a series of sites in the Northern and Western Isles has now revolutionized our perception of the succeeding early historic settlement. Formerly this was unidentifiable, although its presence was attested by certain distinctive artefacts (primarily bone pins and combs). Structures had simply not been recognized in these areas because, in comparison to the preceding monumental Iron Age buildings, they were insubstantial. It can now be seen that many of the older sites continued to be occupied, albeit in modified form, as single farmsteads. Cellular complexes of conjoined roundhouses and attached cells were built within or besides their monumental predecessors, surrounded by or dug into middens and dunes, often utilizing earlier features and undergoing several phases of construction. A wheelhouse at Cnip, Lewis was gradually transformed to a cellular complex, finally to be replaced by a linear house.

Similar architectural forms are also found overlying some Orcadian and Shetland brochs and the nucleated villages which had developed around them (at Gurness, Howe and Upper Scalloway, for example) (36). In some instances these later settlements may have been deliberately sited to exploit the former status of brochs. Rectilinear buildings found on some sites may relate to a series of poorly understood structures in Caithness and Sutherland known as 'wags' (from the Gaelic *uamh* for 'cave') – linear buildings with rounded ends divided internally by pairs of opposing upright stones into stalls.

The new range of building types found on Atlantic roundhouse sites has also been found away from them. Inevitably their slight nature renders them difficult to detect, unless recognized during the course of coastal erosion. At Buckquoy (see 30) a single building with a so-called 'figure-of-eight' or linear arrangement of sub-circular cells was found, and this type of plan appears to have had a wide currency. A complex of buildings with similar plans, perhaps a village, has apparently been found on the Udal in the Western Isles, but this still awaits publication. At Deer Park Farm in Northern Ireland the construction of a timber equivalent has been precisely dated by dendrochronology to after 648.

At Pool on the Orcadian island of Sanday, an extensive network of interconnecting buildings

**36** *Reconstruction of 'Shamrock', Gurness, Orkney; this Pictish building is so named because of its distinctive ground-plan.*

set into a Neolithic midden was excavated in the 1980s. The first structures were a souterrain-type feature and building with bins along two sides, apparently for feeding animals. In the fifth century, or so it is argued, a stone roundhouse was built and subsequently remodelled. It had a partial ring of low upright stones which encircled an inner area containing a hearth; the outer ring was divided into a series of radial divisions, some of which contained tanks for storage. The presence of post-holes, sockets and pads attests to the use of timber, which must then have been a more widely available commodity than it is now. In the sixth century a second chamber was added, while subsequently a rectangular courtyard was created and used for the dumping of midden material. A large area of paving gave

access to the buildings around it. This deliberate expansion must have involved considerable social organization, but the settlement ultimately contracted in size, to be taken over by the Vikings in the eighth century.

It is also thought that some of the farmmounds traditionally dated to *c.* 800, which have a restricted distribution in parts of Orkney and the coast of Norway, may have had a seventh-century origin. Nothing is known about the precise nature of this early settlement type, but the mounds appear to have accumulated due to the build-up of organic wastes (such as peat ash) which, for some reason, were not being distributed to the fields as fertilizer.

Before leaving the Pictish periphery, we should consider why the transition from monumental Atlantic roundhouses to less substantial cellular structures appears to coincide with changes in the nature of settlement *throughout* Scotland. Dating is poor but suggests a transformation in the fourth or fifth century AD with little evidence of a break in settlement. So to what can this be attributed? The possible role of the Romans has already been mentioned (see above), but this is an unsatisfactory answer and we need to look to before their advent in the British Isles to consider how these settlements first came to be built.

Analysis of settlement architecture can provide important insights into the development of society because buildings are the places where most human action and interaction is likely to take place. Without going into too much detail (see *Celtic Scotland*, this series), it can be suggested that Atlantic roundhouses developed from native settlement prototypes (and not due to foreign invasion or migration, as used to be thought) as a means of expressing authority and closely controlling the activities of inhabitants. The more impressive the appearance of a settlement the higher its perceived status. The widespread nature of these settlements suggests that power largely resided at the local, extended family-group level. But architecture is only one means by which power can be expressed and, as relations of clientship gradually began to supersede kinship, society became more centralized. Authority was relocated from the immediate settlement to, with regard to most of the farming population, more remote power centres. In the case of the Pictish periphery, its inhabitants were becoming part of a wider confederacy of peoples, the ultimate leader of which was first based north – subsequently south – of the Mounth, in the Pictish heartlands. Since ultimate authority no longer existed within the immediate family group, alternative expressions of power other than architecture (which had most impact on its residents) came into play. As we shall see below, the control of resources, particularly prestige goods, became very important. Personal appearance and the capacity to display wealth to people whom one did not see on a day-to-day basis became a much more important and effective means of demonstrating authority.

This was a portable, symbolic code which could be understood over far-flung areas.

We have demonstrated how the development of the monumental roundhouses (duns) of Argyll and subsequent architectural forms appear to reflect political developments as well as providing evidence for the nature of the farming communities themselves. Dating evidence suggests origins from the late first millennium BC, but there is also enough artefactual evidence to suggest that later occupation was also taking place on these sites. Whether the majority of these duns were being built in the centuries on either side of 700 AD cannot be demonstrated, and on balance may be unlikely, although we know that stout timber and stone defences of dun-like proportions form the core of some early historic power centres (Chapter 3). Outworks discovered around many of the Argyll duns might conceivably relate to early historic settlement.

## Farms and estates

All available evidence suggests that both Pictland and Argyll were divided into large units of land. Within these individual households, services and tribute were owed, via the intermediary of estates (a group of units), to potentates who lived in or ruled from regional power centres. In Argyll these potentates would have been the king or a member of the aristocracy; in Pictland, from the eighth century, these might also have included appointed officials. These units were the means by which assessments for military service, and the equivalents of cain (a regular tribute on all territories acknowledging a king's superiority) and conveth (an obligation of hospitality – food or accommodation) could be made. Together these would have formed the main sources of revenue for the crown.

Study of early medieval (and later) kingship in the British Isles has demonstrated how kings and their courts had to keep on the move to survive, for it made more sense for them to go

37 *Pictish stone showing a hunting scene (in St Vigean's Museum).*

associated with the elite, was probably also an integral part of these tours (37, **back cover**); highly structured activities such as division of spoils and communal feasting reflected the status of the participants. In this way relations of dependency would have been reinforced. Obviously there was a physical limit to how far away and how frequently a king or queen might visit their whole kingdom. Tax in kind from the periphery of kingdoms is therefore likely to have been livestock sent on the hoof or non-perishable goods, such as candles, fleece and hides. A network of loyal, royal officials, each probably with his own circuit, was therefore essential if royalty was to retain some form of authority, however nominal, over larger territories. What then is the evidence for estates and the collection of agricultural resources?

The *Senchus fer nAlban* was compiled to inform an overking, or an outside authority, how much tribute could be expected from the Dál Riata. The number of taxable households within each kindred is itemized, as is the number of men each could provide for military expeditions. On the basis of parallels in Ireland and contemporary Britain, this document demonstrates that the primary economically viable unit was the individual household and associated lands, and that this was the unit on which the raising of rent, tax or tribute was based. These units (likely to have been occupied by the equivalent of base clients) were grouped together in units of five to form what we might refer to as 'townships' or 'estates', run by a lesser noble. Comparison of the detailed accounts of household land divisions in Islay (as described in the *Senchus*) and the distribution of surviving contemporary settlement does not enable us to relate the field remains to the type of pattern implied by the survey. However, it is clear that sophisticated mechanisms existed for the collection of tribute in Argyll, and this also implies the existence of assemblies for the purpose of assessing these burdens (probably at, or near, power centres).

to the food, rather than vice versa. They did this by visiting their own land (on a seasonal basis) and obtaining food renders from its inhabitants, or by taking hospitality from a magnate or monastery. Hence the food requirements of the expensive court were successfully divided across the kingdom. Such journeys were important not only because they sustained the court but because relations of control and clientship were physically reinforced by the royal presence. There was the opportunity for royalty to meet their subjects, to bestow on them prestige goods, to dispense justice and to collect tribute. Hunting, an activity especially

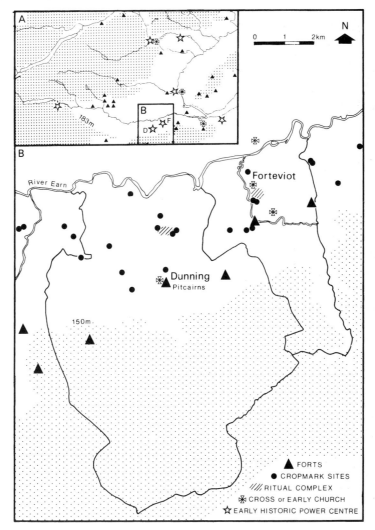

38 *Thanages of Dunning and Forteviot, based on old parish boundaries (conjectural).*

Like most of their neighbours, it is probable that the Picts collected tax and tribute too. In comparison to Argyll, much of Pictland would have been of high agricultural potential and the evidence suggests, as we might therefore expect, the early development of sophisticated mechanisms for dealing with this: the pre-feudal shire called, in later times, thanages. It is suggested that each thanage had three components: a *caput*, or principal royal residence; a series of important major farms which constitute the *pett* ('dependent estate') recognized from place-name evidence (Chapter 2); and a ceremonial centre which served as a meeting-place where popular courts and inauguration ceremonies could be held. The estates were run by free clients, who

had oversight of a number of dependent farms, run by base clients. Shared facilities, such as water-mills, may been sited at the principal residences. Forms of administration based on the principle of the 'multiple-estate' (composed of several units) are found throughout post-Roman Britain under many names.

Using a combination of archaeological and historical evidence, it is possible to suggest the extent of some thanages and to identify the key components within each (38). Unfortunately it is impossible to identify the individual farmsteads without excavation of some of the ubiquitous crop-mark remains in these areas. This bottom-up approach demonstrates that power flowed into the hands of the royal and religious authorities by means of a thoroughly structured and organized landscape of agricultural exploitation.

It is clear that even if the boundaries and internal structure of the predecessors of thanages did not change (which is unlikely), the people in charge of them did. The extension of royal authority to new areas must also mean that authorities acquired, through either passive or aggressive means, the right to make grants of land outside their own territories. The transfer of land, whether to the Church or individuals, must have brought with it major

**39** *Mould for an escutcheon from Craig Phádraig (66mm/2½in diam.) similar to a manufactured example from Castle Tioram. Both sites are interpreted as early historic power centres. The mould suggests that some hanging bowls (which date from the mid-sixth to late seventh century and beyond) were being made in Scotland (NMS).*

changes in the fabric of society. Gifts of land or transfer for their responsibility went in one direction only, resulting in a permanent obligation to the giver which could never be discharged. The officials who acquired this delegated responsibility in return for their loyalty would have striven to uphold the system from which their source of wealth derived and which it was in their interest to succour. Conversely, there was always the danger that if they were given too much power they might abuse it and turn against the hand which fed them: endowment of land and/or its associated privileges was a risky, but necessary move.

## Specialized activities

The power of potentates did not extend purely from the effective way in which they collected and consumed agricultural produce and other local trade, although this was the most important aspect of exchange. All the evidence points to them having used their surplus resources to support a range of specialized activities and hence to control the production and/or distribution of prestige goods. In turn these goods were used to win further clients, hence accelerating the process of taking – probably by violent means – since leaders required more to give away. In the absence of a monetary economy, manipulation of these goods was an important means of establishing new elites, and extending authority over increasingly greater distances. Specialized craftworkers, particularly fine-metalworkers, appear to have largely confined their activities to high-status sites where their food requirements were provided by clients, leaving them free to ply their trade (**39**). The peripheral areas of sites appear to have been reserved for such industrial purposes. From Dunadd, for example, there is evidence for specialized crucibles for gold and silver, the presence of top-quality Anglo-Saxon gold and garnet work, moulds for the manufacture of brooches related to the famous Tara brooch (now in the National Museum of Ireland, Dublin) and

1  Book of Kells: *Christ enthroned and attended by angels. At one time this manuscript had an ornate gold cover (perhaps a gift from a ninth- or tenth-century royal donor) but this was stolen in 1007 (the Board of Trinity College Dublin).*

2 *Dundurn fort, Perthshire.*

3 *Forteviot, crop marks. The main palace is believed to have stood in the immediate vicinity (RCAHMS).*

4 *Easter Kinnear, Fife. Scooped houses, part of a nucleated, unenclosed settlement of the mid-first millennium* AD, *during the course of excavation. The feature on the right represents a sequence in which roundhouses were finally replaced by a timber, rectangular building (RCAHMS).*

5 *Falconry scene on the reverse of a cross-slab within the grounds of Elgin Cathedral.*

6 *Hunterston brooch, found in the early nineteenth century in Ayrshire. It was manufactured during the late seventh or early eighth century, very possibly in Argyll. Its central panel incorporates a prominent cross motif. Described as one of the finest products of the Celtic goldsmith's art, its form and decoration owe much to both Celtic and Anglo-Saxon traditions (NMS).*

7  *Some finds from the St Ninian's Isle treasure:*
   *bowl, brooches, mounts and chapes (NMS).*

8 Reconstruction of feasting in an early historic hall.

9 Class I slab from Dairy Park, Dunrobin. The symbols include a mirror, comb, snake and Z-rod.

10 A rare example of an upstanding Pictish cemetery at Whitebridge, Inverness-shire (Robert Gourlay, Highland Regional Council).

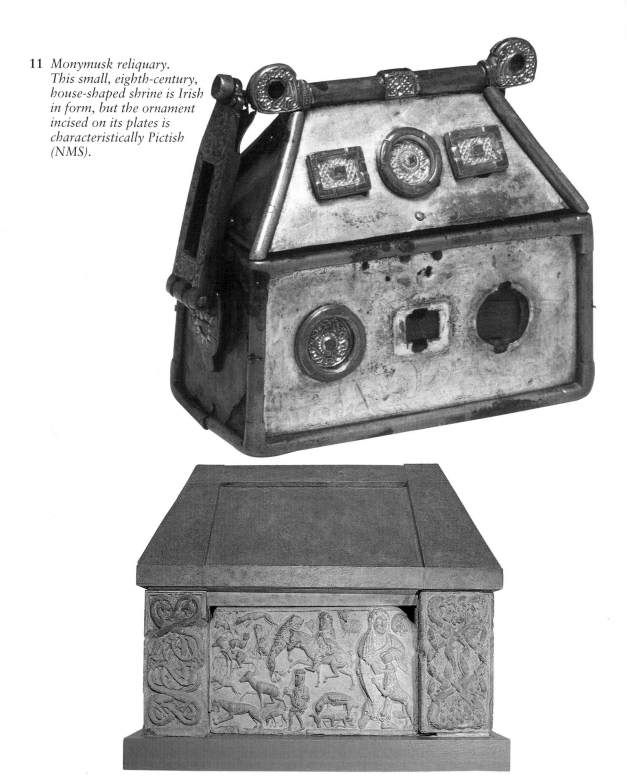

11 *Monymusk reliquary. This small, eighth-century, house-shaped shrine is Irish in form, but the ornament incised on its plates is characteristically Pictish (NMS).*

12 *Sarcophagus from St Andrews (now reconstructed with a flat top). The iconography refers to King David, and may allude to the themes of conversion and salvation. Although inspiration may have come from foreign models, many elements of the design have been modified to a native style. Four corner slabs were slotted vertically to receive flanged end and side panels; corner-post shrines from elsewhere in Pictland, e.g. Shetland, appear also to be native in form.*

40 *Mould for a bird-headed brooch from Dunadd (RCAHMS).*

41 *Sculpted cross on the island of Canna. The person on the bottom left, dressed in contemporary fashion, is wearing a penannular brooch (RCAHMS).*

Hunterston brooch (see **colour plate 6**), and moulds for the production of brooches with bird heads and interlace (Celtic in form but Anglo-Saxon in style) (**40**). In the meantime the potentates were able to employ their excess material resources and physical energies in a wide range of exclusive activities, such as horse breeding (the outer enclosures at some forts may have been for their stabling), falconry (**colour plate 5**), hunting and preparation for military campaigns. Training and management of the horse would have required the services of grooms, as well as large quantities of fodder.

Among the fine objects produced by the metalworkers on these sites are seventh- and eighth-century penannular and annular brooches which Irish law tracts and earlier British poetry suggest would have been worn in Scotland and Ireland as status symbols. Sculpture shows them to have been worn singly, either on the shoulder (for men) or breast (women) (**41**). This idea may have been adopted from the late Roman use of brooches as insignia of office. It might even have been an attempt to draw on Roman traditions of social organization and power in order to assert the legitimacy of their early historic owners. Gift giving was an important means of distributing largess in a non-monetary economy and so, by controlling the production of these brooches, the potentates were able to reinforce their social positions. In this way prestige goods might be used to dissolve old tribal structures and establish new elites. They could achieve this by determining who they might give such status symbols to and from

whom, in return, they could expect or extract loyalty and services. Gift giving had very much a contractual character in this period and objects of value could also be used to promote or seal political alliances.

The secular status of these brooches would appear to have been adopted by the higher echelons of the Church, whose members often came from the aristocracy. The brooches also incorporate decorative elements drawing on Christian iconography (**colour plate 6**) (although some of this is open to multiple interpretations). They would therefore have conveyed a Christian message to their wearer (whether a cleric or not) while the implied status was a motif understood by all ranks of society. Given the Church's role in legitimizing the status of potentates at this time (Chapter 5), the inclusion of Christian iconography in jewellery was a graphic statement of this relationship.

The existence of enormous wealth is exemplified by both individual works of art and treasures such as those from St Ninian's Isle, Burgar and Norrie's Law. There must have been enormous competition to procure the services of the craftspeople who possessed these superlative artistic and technical skills.

## Norrie's Law hoard, Fife

Very little survives of what was once a very large hoard of silver objects found in 1819 at the foot of a prehistoric cairn. The amount of silver available in Pictland is exceptional, and may have related to access to sources of late Roman silver. Deposited in the second half of the seventh century (perhaps during Northumbrian claims to overlordship of the area), the remaining finds from Norrie's Law include: three pins (one decorated with a Pictish symbol), two penannular brooches, a pair of unique plaques (both decorated with Pictish symbols: **42**), a bossed disc, folded Roman spoons (scrap metal) and a late Iron Age embossed disc. Little credence can be given to the supposed inclusion of a shield, helmet and

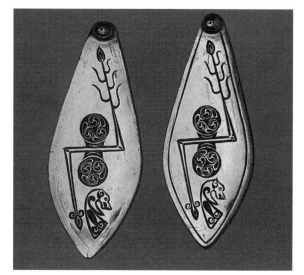

42 *Two finds from the Norrie's Law hoard: silver plaques with incised decoration picked out in red enamel (NMS).*

sword, although some fragments of silver plate may be the covering from a round parade shield. The hoard therefore includes material spanning a very wide age range.

## St Ninian's Isle treasure, Shetland

This hoard was discovered in 1958 under a stone slab in the east end of a medieval church where excavation demonstrated the existence of an important early Christian foundation. Interpreted as secular, or the secular portion of a rich treasury buried c. 800 due to Viking raids, the hoard comprised 28 decorated silver objects and the jawbone of a porpoise placed in a larch box: 8 bowls (one a hanging bowl), probably tableware; a spoon and another implement; a sword pommel and 2 elaborate sword chapes (one with a dedication (see **80**), the only metalwork early historic sword-fittings from Scotland); 3 cone-shaped mounts (for attachment to a sword-belt?) and 12 penannular brooches (**colour plate 7**). The style of the metalwork led to the recognition of a distinctive style of brooch with lentoid heads and raised cusps (see **12**) which is described as Pictish because it is largely found in north and west Scotland. However, new finds, such as from Carronbridge in south-west Scotland, suggest a wider distribution.

## Broch of Burgar hoard, Orkney

In about the 1840s a remarkable hoard of up to eight silver vessels was found 'in the thickness of the wall' of one of the intramural cells of Broch of Burgar. One vessel was nearly filled with several silver combs of varying sizes, five or six silver pins, several fragments of silver chain and a large number of amber beads. Alas none of the hoard now survives, but in the absence of coins it can be presumed to have been either Viking or Pictish (rather than late Roman), while the general range of artefacts suggests it may in fact be an eighth-century Pictish treasure, deposited when the Vikings began to raid the area. The bowl is described third-hand in 1859 (in not very good English!) as 'beautifully ornamented apparently stamped on it and also having numerous projecting knobs on it' and there is the exciting possibility that this connects it to the so-called 'boss style' well known in late eighth-century metalwork and sculpture throughout Scotland, but particularly Pictland (**43, front cover**). Although it cannot be conclusively proved that this assemblage was Pictish, it seems beyond reasonable doubt that the artefacts would have once formed the property of a wealthy Orcadian. The amber (presumably from the east coast of England, or perhaps farther afield in the Baltic) highlights the extent of trading contacts.

In addition to the production of such splendid and overtly ornate objects, there was also an increasing tendency to mass-produce smaller pieces of jewellery. These were needed to enable more frequent gifts to be given to the expanding number of followers which a potentate could hope to obtain. In addition to jewellery, the metalworkers could also have made ornate drinking horns, harness pieces, weapon-fittings, as well as more 'mundane' items such as decorated vessels or furniture.

We might also expect these sites to have possessed smiths (as at Dunadd), high-status craftspeople who forged agricultural implements and weapons. Survival conditions dictate that very little evidence has been found for either of these, but both were essential. Swords, like brooches, were also very important gifts for potentates to be able to bestow on their followers, as the heroic poems of the time emphasize. Horse gear is also likely to have been an important product of both the smith and fine-metalworker although, unlike in Ireland, surprisingly little direct evidence survives for this.

## Trade

Power centres controlled local trade, and hence they were located at nodal points in the landscape, such as river-crossings, where they could control the movement of people, collecting taxes as appropriate. In Argyll (and Strathclyde) some of them also controlled the acquisition and distribution of imported goods, which are found in western Britain and Ireland from the late fifth century to early eighth (**44**). Four main types of imported pottery have been

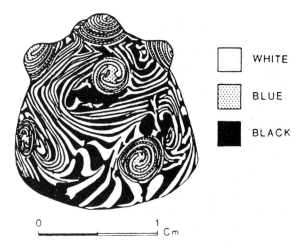

WHITE

BLUE

BLACK

0    1 Cm

**43** *Glass boss from Dundurn, of the eighth or ninth century, likely to have decorated a fine piece of metalwork, perhaps a reliquary (Leslie and Elizabeth Alcock; Society of Antiquaries of Scotland).*

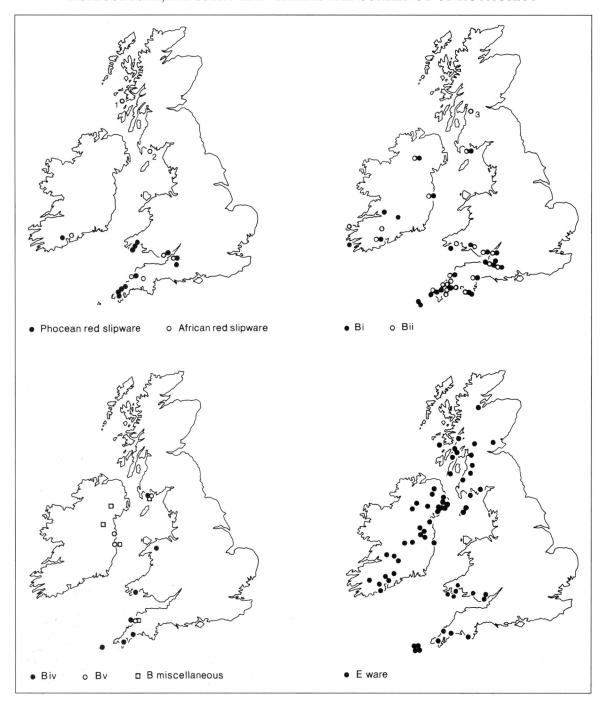

**44** *Distribution of imported pottery in the British Isles: 1 Iona; 2 Whithorn; 3 Dumbarton Rock.*

identified: A, B, D and E ware ('C' was discovered to be medieval some time ago). The total number of vessels throughout the British Isles is still small, but from these, two successive trading systems have been identified.

Firstly, between the late fifth to mid-sixth century there was a brief period of direct trading with the eastern Mediterranean. Various types of amphorae and jars (Bi from the

Peloponnese; Bii from south-east Turkey; Biv from Sardis, Asia Minor; and Bvi from Gaza) and bowls (Phocean red slip ware from Asia Minor and the Aegean) were brought to south-west Britain, probably via North Africa where various other amphorae (Bv from Tunisia) and late Roman bowls (African red slip ware from Carthage) were added to the cargo. The amphorae were primarily containers for liquids, such as olive-oil and wine. These Mediterranean traders appear to have taken back with them metal: tin from Cornwall, and lead and silver from the Mendips and south Wales. Certain coastal forts (Tintagel in Cornwall, Cadbury Congresbury in Somerset and Dinas Powys in Wales) appear to have been major (presumably seasonal) trading centres, although significant but undefended sites are now also beginning to enter the equation and may have been trading under royal control, if they were not royal themselves. The small groups of sherds discovered in Scotland may simply represent redistribution from south-west Britain as a result of social and political links. On the other hand, the presence of a single sherd of African red slip ware from Iona may simply emphasize the importance of this particular monastery and the exceptional breadth of its contacts. The nature of the goods being traded from Scotland can only be

guessed at – white furs, river pearls and rock crystal have been suggested, but more prosaic items such as woollen textiles or leather products, perhaps even hunting dogs (recorded as a British export by Strabo 500 years beforehand) or slaves are equally probable. An exquisitely carved wooden box from Evie in Orkney confirms the skills of the woodworker, while its contents were the tools of a leatherworker whose labours would probably have ranged from the production of shields, saddles, vellum and bridles to clothing (**45**). No doubt many of these formed part of the tribute which potentates demanded from their clients. This trading system ceased, perhaps when the Byzantine empire reimposed control over the western Mediterranean.

A second system appeared in the later sixth century and seventh (with minor activity only in the early eighth century). Mortaria and bowls (D ware, from the Bordeaux region), tableware and storage vessels (E ware, exact provenance unknown) were brought from Gaul, along with imported glass drinking vessels to the Irish Sea zone. Glass vessels are also known to have existed from the documentary sources: the *Gododdin* refers to 'the wine of brimming glass vessels' and Columba caused the glass held by King Bridei's magician to shatter. Distant trade should not surprise us,

45 *Carved wooden box from Evie, Orkney*
*(29cm/11½in long) (NMS).*

for Adomnán describes the visit of Gaulish merchants between 565 and 597, and other sources also attest to regular contact between Gaul and the western British Isles during this period. A Frankish brooch from Dunadd may also relate to such contacts. The south-west of England was largely excluded from this trading cycle, perhaps because much of it was now under English control.

The E ware (which contained exotic goods such as dye) was almost certainly a space-filler for a cargo of wine in timber barrels. Together the wine, tableware and glass drinking vessels illustrate the importance which potentates placed on feasting (**colour plate 8**). The perishable nature of such a cargo serves to remind us how much trade is simply invisible. E ware comes in a wide variety of forms and it appears that there is a major discrepancy in the type of vessel found at major centres such as Dunadd and the lesser dun and crannog sites within a 80km (50 mile) radius. This appears to imply differential patterns of distribution as a reflection of political relations rather than trade.

Reliance on the seaways for communication and trade is reflected in the coastal distribution of many of the early historic power centres, in contrast to earlier defended sites of the Iron Age. Indeed, some may have been sited on the coast in a conscious attempt to control the availability of imported luxury goods. Ultimately this control may have been too strong because when northern European ports began to take over continental trade, and towns were founded in England (such as *Hamwic*, modern Southampton), proto-towns failed to emerge in Scotland. Elsewhere, kings sanctioned neutral places where trading could flourish. St Andrews is the only Scottish town which developed from a known Pictish power

centre, but the extent to which its early role involved trading can only be guessed.

Pictland's trading contacts are likely to have been primarily along the east coast, particularly with Northumbria, but perhaps as far afield as Frisia. A leaf-shaped spearhead found in the post-broch levels at Upper Scalloway is thought to be a sixth- or seventh-century import from Kent.

Secular power centres were therefore often strategically sited, symbolic manifestations of the authority and power of their inhabitants. But it is clear that they were primarily focal points for the collection, transformation and redistribution of tax and tribute from which potentates derived their wealth and much of their authority. Control of local trade was particularly important, since some of these resources were used to produce prestige goods or were exchanged for imports used in the course of the royal activities of feasting and gift giving. Yet the power centres did not exist in a vacuum but were part of a structured network of royal and noble sites through which agricultural wealth could be exploited. The early historic period saw the development of the means to extract such surplus from the land. Broad similarities exist between Pictland and Argyll, which should not surprise us given their proximity and close political interrelationship. Each area seems to have developed a sophisticated division of land and associated administration, but the greater agricultural wealth of Pictland may have precipitated a complex mechanism for this.

It is now time to turn to the evidence for the early Church, which not only played an active part in the early historic economy, but provided the ideological backbone to many of the social and political developments of the age.

# CHAPTER FIVE

# The strength of belief

Christianity was the most significant force of change during the early historic period. By the early tenth century most people would have been familiar with Christian beliefs. Certainly none could have ignored the impact of its ideology or the might of its messengers. Its leaders were major landowners, effectively secular potentates in all but name. Very often they came from important families and their actions, however they might be packaged, were closely tied to the politics of the time. The point at which the aims and aspirations of the secular and religious elites gelled therefore marks a crucial stage in the development of kingship and the Scottish nation. The Church became a powerful ambassador for the kings with whom it worked to shape and nurture the ideal of a Christian ruler. The extent to which Christianity permeated the rural lay population dictated how effectively such messages might be conveyed. The clerics also brought with them the technology of writing, over which they had a virtual monopoly. The potential of literacy to create a 'power-jump' – radically to affect the means by which society operated – cannot be underestimated.

What we therefore need to examine is the inter-relationship between the Church, secular authorities and the rural population, and the role of literacy. But first, we must review pagan beliefs.

## Pre-Christian beliefs

Pagan Celts believed in a pantheon of gods and a supernatural 'other-world'; trees, hills, water, the sun and animals (wild, domesticated and fabulous) were all sacred to them, supported by an imaginative and colourful mythology. We should envisage an annual round of festivities which was closely tied to the agricultural cycle and the concept of fertility. In contrast to their continental and British neighbours, relatively little is known of actual religious practice, but it is clear that the sacrifice of animals took place, probably in association with feasting, followed by the ritual deposition of parts of their carcasses in pits. Votive deposits of Iron Age metalwork including, in the south of Scotland, Roman objects, appear to shed some light on Pictish pagan practices, specifically the invention and widespread use of certain designs, the so-called 'Pictish symbols'.

## Pictish symbols

A unique range of at least fifty designs (**46**), familiarly referred to as 'symbols', have been found incised on undressed stones (up to 206 examples which archaeologists refer to as Class I), cave walls or rock outcrops (6 examples), silver jewellery or miscellaneous objects. Some of these same designs have also been found carved in relief on 63 dressed stones (Class II) which include Christian iconography and originate in the late seventh/early eighth century (see below). These designs might also have been used in other media: wood, leather and textiles and

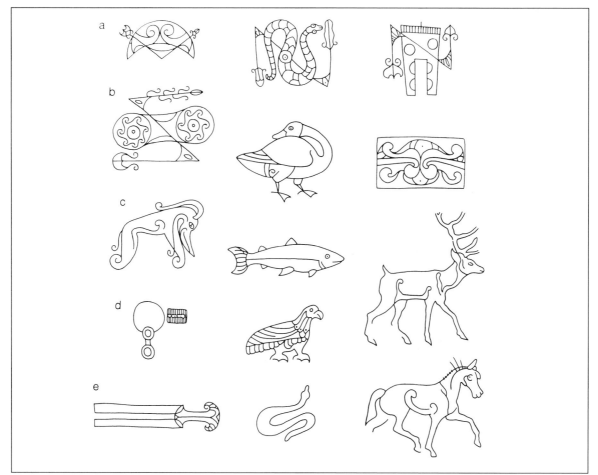

**46** *Examples of Pictish symbols:* (a) *crescent and V-rod;* (b) *double disc and Z-rod;* (c) *Pictish beast;* (d) *mirror and comb;* (e) *sword.*

body decoration. Class I and II stones are found almost exclusively in Pictland (**47**). Most are confined to the fertile lowlands of the east coast, with Class I predominating to the north of the Mounth, Class II to the south. Only three of the designs have a widespread distribution or occur more than twenty times: the so-called crescent (see **46a**); double disc (see **46b**); and the Pictish beast / 'swimming elephant' (see **46c**). The crescent is often overlain by a 'V-rod' and the double disc by a 'Z-rod' (which sometimes overlies other symbols), but never the other way round. The crescent and double disc are often singled out for the most elaborate decoration (**48**). With the exception of some animals, the

designs are almost always paired, and in a fifth to a quarter of cases are accompanied by representations of a mirror and comb (see **46d**), often at the base of a series of designs.

Interpretation of the meaning of the individual symbols, the function of the objects which carry them and their date continues to excite furious debate. Individual symbols have been identified as totemic symbols of lineage; indicators of rank, clan and profession; or components of personal names. The Class I stones are therefore seen as memorials to the dead (although not necessarily placed over the corpses); testimonies to marriage alliances between matrilineal clans; statements of tribal affiliation; or charters in stone, erected by descendants to legitimize their inheritance of land. However, used over several centuries and in many different situations (not just carved stones) the designs cannot be strait-jacketed;

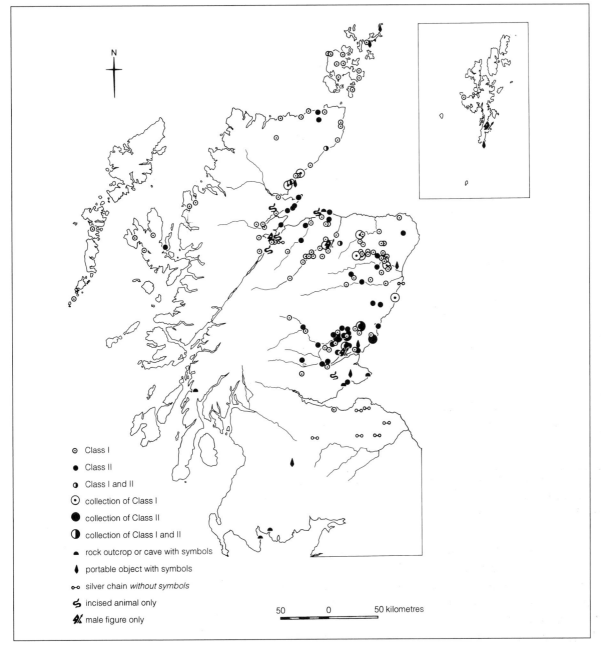

N

Class I ⊙
Class II ●
Class I and II ◑
collection of Class I ⊙
collection of Class II ●
collection of Class I and II ◑
rock outcrop or cave with symbols
portable object with symbols
silver chain *without symbols* ∘∘
incised animal only
male figure only

50    0    50 kilometres

**47** *Distribution of Pictish early sculpture and associated artwork.*

identical motifs may have meant something different in each context, although their repertoire demonstrates shared and widespread beliefs. They appear to make most sense when looked at in the light of Celtic religious beliefs and practices.

It is argued here that the designs were used in situations where they affirmed and enhanced the status of the elite and respect for the gods

(Chapter 3). The designs evoke aspects of Celtic religious practice, belief which associated power (through ritual) specifically with leaders. This association with high-status people and their activities is reflected in several ways: the nature and content of the symbolism; the

73

**48** *Pictish beast, double disc, Z-rod and other symbols on a Class II stone from Brodie. The ogham inscription around this stone is so damaged by weathering that few of its 70 or so characters can now be read (Tom Gray).*

using a grid to lay out the design), mostly identifiable as the domestic and wild animals which the Celts are known to have revered, even if they are not the ones most commonly illustrated elsewhere in the Celtic world. The most common of these is the 'Pictish beast', apparently a dolphin or perhaps the fantastic kelpie or waterhorse of later Scottish folklore. Unlike the other designs, the animals are sometimes depicted singly, notably the thirty or so bull plaques from Burghead for which a cult status has been attributed (Chapter 3; see **22a**). Each animal traditionally possessed specific attributes and associations which their artists may have been trying to evoke.

About seventeen of the designs have been tentatively identified as abstract representations of high-status objects which had a currency in north Britain between the first and third centuries: sword (see **46e**), harness-ring, cauldron, anvil, tongs, mirror, comb, brooch and armlet, for example. It is striking that many of these are the types of objects which we know to have been placed in Scottish Iron Age votive offerings or northern British burials. The Z-rod and V-rod have been interpreted as representations of broken and bent spears and arrows, perhaps referring to the northwest European ritual practice of breaking weapons before deposition in order to release their strength to another world.

The style of the mirror has parallels in Iron Age Britain, including a complete mirror from Balmaclellan, Kirkcudbright, but the comb is very unusual since at least three forms are known and, unlike the other symbols, they appear to represent updated models of the objects which they depict: a later form of comb is represented on Class II stones. Mirror and comb are conventionally interpreted as 'female' signifiers, but the arguments are weak and largely based on modern, male-oriented views. Although at Hilton of Cadboll a mirror and comb have been juxtaposed next to one of the few representations of a female in early Scottish art, and the slab overlying the woman

objects which the designs are found on; and the context in which these objects are used. Given the apparent relationship to religious beliefs, much of which pivoted around the sacral role of kings, the appropriation of these designs in wide-ranging contexts (at whatever date) becomes easier to understand *without* necessarily having to comprehend their precise, individual meaning.

Throughout Britain and north-west Europe animals were carved because of their religious and symbolic value. Many of the designs are naturalistic animals (carefully depicted, possibly buried at Dunrobin Dairy Park (**colour plate 9**) did include a mirror and comb, we need only remind ourselves of the importance of long hair and moustaches to male status to see that sole female associations cannot be justified.

Despite their patent ability to depict familiar subjects naturalistically, many symbols can only be characterized as abstract designs which therefore have no identifiable link with pagan beliefs and practices, although their designs generally evoke styles of ornament prevalent on Iron Age metalwork. Such objects – whether during their circulation or final deposition – reflected the personal wealth of their elite owners through whom the identity and status of the wider community was personified. Although ritual pervaded all aspects of life, we might expect use of these arcane Pictish designs to only have been sanctioned by those with knowledge of their mysterious and secret significance. This becomes clearer when we look at the circumstances in which they were used.

North of the Mounth it has been observed that Class I stones have a tendency to cluster close to conspicuous prehistoric ritual sites, notably stone circles and henges, indicating either a cult centre and/or centre of population (**49**). Sometimes, as at Ardlair, Brandsbutt and Edderton, the symbols have been drawn directly on to prehistoric standing stones. The Picts may therefore have been deliberately trying to associate themselves with monuments of past significance and in doing so they created places in which their own rituals could be enacted and, as in prehistoric times, where direct access to certain sacred places may have been restricted and the types of activities which could take place there were socially proscribed. An increasing number of Class I stones are now being found to overlie burials, while the discovery of some on sites which later became Christian burial grounds implies continuity of function from a pagan site of worship/burial.

Pictish burial takes a wide variety of forms. Simple inhumations are known but the long cist (a stone/slab-lined rectangular grave), diffi-

**49** *The portrayal of a single human figure (probably derived from pagan myth) is unusual. This carving from Barflat is associated with a cropmark enclosure which originally contained six, possibly eight stones, two of which bear incised figures.*

cult to date in the absence of grave-goods, is the most typical and widespread type. Sometimes the cemeteries may have pagan origins. C-14 dating of skeletons from excavations has determined that some long cists found in north Scotland under platforms of earth or stone, or low stone kerbs (both circular and square in plan), date to between the fourth and eighth centuries. Of these, the square barrows sometimes share a common side and their surrounding ditches are likely to be interrupted at the corners (**colour plate 10**; see **4**). Class I stones have been found in association with a number of these cairns and barrows (at Garbeg, Inverness and Dunrobin, Sutherland), and stone pillars sometimes mark the corners of the cairns. Similar burials known only from crop marks have been found in southern Pictland and, in one instance, Argyll (circular barrows only, see **11**). There is a square barrow and circular enclosure to the immediate north-east of the Collessie stone (see **2**), for example. At Easterton of Roseisle a short cist, which possibly contained a cremation, incorporated a

Class I stone (**50**), as did one of a group of similar undated burials overlying the broch at Oxtro (Orkney), which also included a stone urn.

The majority of extant Pictish designs are on carved stones, the carving of which required enormous technical skills and physical resources that would only have been accessible to the elite. The same applies to the high-quality metalwork on which the designs have also been found. The Norrie's Law hoard (Chapter 4) included a hand-pin for fastening clothing and a pair of identical leaf-shaped plaques (possibly related to Roman votive plaques), both incised with symbols (see **42**). Ten massive silver chains are also known (**51**). The only possible argument for any of the chains being manufactured in Pictland is that two of the terminals are decorated with Pictish designs, but one of these is from south of the Forth, as are the majority of the known chains (see **47**). Virtually nothing is known about their final contexts, but they are likely to have been ritually deposited.

Whatever their context, it therefore seems that Pictish designs were employed to evoke aspects of religious belief and the high-status individuals in control of this. Clearly they mostly survive on accomplished objects or monuments, often standardized in form, whose production and use were confined to the upper echelons of society. The perceived status of the objects themselves, and the symbolic status of the emblems with which they were adorned, seem appropriate given the pivotal and direct role which pagan kings and priests played in intervention with the other-world. Whether they were encountered upon the person of a king, during seasonal festivities or rites of passage (such as death and subsequent transference of inheritance), these designs were employed in situations where they affirmed and enhanced both the status of the elite (who had godly attributes) and respect for the gods (with

50 *A Class I stone from a short cist at Easterton of Roseisle.*

51 *Silver chain with Pictish symbols (48cm/19in long, 1731g/61oz) from Whitecleugh (NMS).*

It becomes very tempting to perceive the most common designs as emblems of royal authority. The lunar, heavenly connotations of the crescent are self-evident. A crescentic bronze plaque from Monifieth Laws, now lost (52), represents the crescent and V-rod with, on its reverse, two other designs. It demonstrates that some designs could exist in their own right. The torc or armlet, symbolized by the double-disc design, might equally have been a symbol of royal authority, likewise the weapons which are used in conjunction with this and the crescent. Did these objects, along with the mirror and comb, relate (however remotely) to certain rites of passage? What are the circumstances which led to the formalization of these permanent and public testimonies; why, where and when did the designs evolve?

whom the elite interceded). In the case of Class I stones, designs symbolize the attributes of individuals who may be buried nearby. But the application of Pictish designs (along with ogham inscriptions) to some 'everyday' items, such as bone pins or stone discs, suggests that their symbolism was not only understood throughout society but applicable in a wide range of contexts, where they were intended to invoke divine intercession in certain tasks. The roughly pecked symbols on a stone slab from Pool, Orkney, were patently not the work of a skilled mason, but they sufficed to mark the construction of a sixth-century house (on the basis of C-14 dating).

The majority of surviving symbols are on Class I and II stones, and it is the currency of Class I which continues both to intrigue and vex. They are presumed to post-date 500, the traditional date for the arrival of the Dál Riata because of their absence in Argyll. One school of thought thinks that they were erected in the fifth/sixth centuries, not long after the circulation of the Iron Age and late Roman objects upon which some designs may be based. But if

52 *Bronze plaque from Monifieth Laws, Angus (front and back). We have no idea how this object might have been used, although it remained in circulation long enough to be highly prized by a Viking who wrote his name on it (114mm/4½in long).*

this is the case, there must be a long passage of time between their advent and subsequent adoption on Class II stones, and on the basis of their artistic treatment this seems untenable. Two further schools of thought exist, and these suggest that they were first erected in the seventh century or from the early eighth century. Both theories revolve around the undeniable relationship between the style of some of the animal symbols and manuscript art: for example, the late seventh-century *Echternach Gospels* (produced in Northumbria at about the same time as the *Lindisfarne Gospels*); and the *Book of Durrow* (from either Northumbria or Iona, depending on which side of 664 it was produced) (see **13**). The arguments are strongest for suggesting that the Northumbrians got their ideas from the Picts, which means that the symbols were already in existence from the mid-seventh century. Class II stones are slightly more firmly dated from the late seventh century or early eighth century.

If the symbols are so much later than the objects which some of them appear to be related to, where did the designs originate? The Pictish artists were clearly well capable of naturalistic depiction of animals they were familiar with, and this surely reinforces the argument that the remaining designs were conceived of and only ever existed in two-dimensional form (the Monifieth plaque falls happily into this category). By the time the Picts came to carve them, the basis of the designs was not fully understood. Several scholars have suggested that the Picts got the idea for Class I stones from Roman sculpture surviving in northern Britain. Parallels can be found here for most of the animals and there is the possibility that the so-called 'mirror' might even be a patera (a round dish with a handle on one side), but this does not explain the origin of the remaining symbols. Alternatively we have to assume that the designs must have been evolving somewhere in an organic medium which does not survive. The long-held and currently unfashionable arguments for Pictish tattooing become tempting. In some parts of Europe and western Asia tattooing was a mark of social status, but until we find the Scottish equivalent of a bog- or ice-person (the 5200-year-old Hauslabjoch man, discovered in 1991 frozen in the Italian Alps, was tattooed) we cannot prove their existence. However, if they did exist, this was one way in which the designs could have been transmitted 'on the hoof' throughout the Pictish confederacy, perhaps as an expression of alliance and unity. But either way, why do they later appear on stone?

Although found throughout Pictland, there are strong art-historical arguments that Class I stones originated around the Moray Firth. Given that this was the power base of Pictland until the seventh century, it is very tempting to see their erection as a form of political statement – even an expression of Pictishness – reflecting the strength of royal authority. The adoption of earlier symbols, redolent with 'national' significance and of a glorious past when the Picts made a marked contribution to the downfall of the Roman empire, could have been an attempt to legitimize a new form of royal authority through the conscious deployment of designs whose earlier significance was still remembered by the population at large.

The growth of the Pictish kingdom and the appearance of this standardized symbolic system apparently occurred at the same time, under the control of a political and/or religious elite. The stones may have been erected to support the establishment of new social positions, which were later to be doubly affirmed on Class II stones by the juxtaposition of the symbols with images of the elite who held those posts. The designs reflect the wider religious/political beliefs of the local community who accepted a social structure in which certain powerful individuals had authority, and under whose influence, if not physical presence, these monuments were erected. Some form of external stress might have precipitated the circumstances in which Class I stones developed, over a period of time, into a widely accepted and understood mode of political expression.

If a historical context is sought for this, we might look to the reigns of Bridei mac Máelchú (died c. 585), king of at least northern Pictland, and his immediate descendants. The stones lack Christian iconography and may have been erected as a pagan reaction against the influence of these new beliefs, whether due to the successes of the sub-Roman or the Columban Church.

## Sub-Roman Church in Pictland

The Columban Church was not the first to introduce Christianity to Pictland. Bede recorded a tradition that Nynia had introduced Christianity to the southern Picts. Very little is known about this saint, although he appears to have been sent to the see of Whithorn (Galloway) during the fifth century to be bishop of a Christian community which had developed from a late Roman-period trading settlement. Various strands of evidence suggest that he and his followers were active in Scotland (largely south of the Antonine Wall). Evidence for a sub-Roman Church, organized on the basis of dioceses with bishops, is found in the surviving distribution of *eccles-* place-names, which imply important early churches related to secular centres (53). An inscribed stone from Peebles refers to a bishop, and there are long-cist cemeteries in the coastal tracts on both sides of the Forth, around the Fife coast and the Tay estuary. A large long-cist cemetery at Hallow Hill, on the edge of modern St Andrews, can be equated with *Eglesnamin*. Although excavation has not located the church, it has produced the only known Pictish road (54). At Kirkliston (Edinburgh airport) a long-cist cemetery was centred around the Catstane, a late sixth-century inscription. It therefore appears that some of the southern Picts received Christianity before the appearance of the Columban Church in Scotland.

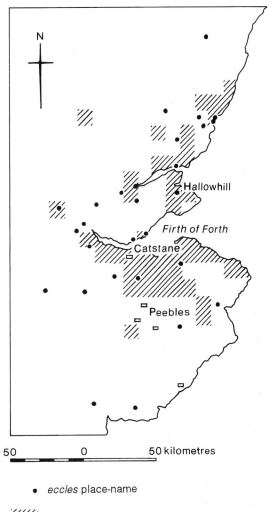

eccles place-name

long-cist burial area

early inscription

53 *Distribution of* eccles- *place-names, long-cist burials and early inscriptions in south-east Scotland.*

## The Columban Church

Although some of the Dál Riata may have been converted beforehand, Christianity first makes its mark in western Scotland with the arrival of Columba in 563. Later to become a saint, he was an important member of the Irish Uí Néill tribe who chose to lead a mission to Scotland in penance for misdemeanours. Based first at

**54** *Hallow Hill, one side of a road with child and adult long-cist burials on either side (Edwina Proudfoot, St Andrews Heritage Services).*

*Hinba* (probably on Jura), within a few years he had moved to Iona, subsequently to become the most important early Christian monastery in Argyll (**55**). Its significance stemmed from Columba's social status and both the enthusiasm and successes of his followers. Iona became a renowned centre of learning and artistic excellence, its most famous product being the *Book of Kells* (see **colour plate 1**). The monastery's international contacts were unsurpassed: it played a leading role in the conversion of Northumbria; was one of the most important Irish religious centres; and ultimately gained supremacy over the Pictish Church in the mid-ninth century.

Christianity was brought to Ireland by the Palladian mission in the first half of the fifth century when, at the request of the pope, several bishops appear to have been active in Ireland under the initial leadership of Palladius. However, Patrick (died 493), whose mission began in the 460s, has tended to be given credit for much of this. The early Irish Church was organized on the basis of dioceses (ecclesiastical territories under the care of a bishop), but Patrick encouraged the monastic ideal (of monks living a religious life, bound by vows and in obedience to a rule under the care of an abbot). Monasticism was the primary factor by the late sixth century, but overall there was not a uniform pattern and a clear distinction cannot be drawn between the two types of organization. Such diversity was apparently also the case in Argyll, as we shall see.

It was the monastic ideal which Columba and his followers brought to Scotland. Iona, a small but fertile island off the west tip of Mull, was granted to them by the king. The setting was obviously intended to be remote; it was later disdainfully referred to by Bishop Wilfrid of Ripon (and reported by Bede) as 'one remote corner of the most remote island ... isolated at the uttermost ends of the earth'. Conall mac Comgaill of the Cenél nGabhráin may have granted this land in a deliberate move to emphasize his authority over neighbouring Loairn, where Iona is situated. Adomnán provides a vivid account of life on Iona, which can be complemented by the surviving field remains and evidence from small-scale excavations (56a). The development of the monastery is scarcely understood, but at its greatest may have been up to 8ha (20 acres) in extent. A rectilinear vallum with rounded corners defined a symbolic and legal boundary. Much of its ditch with inner and outer banks can still be traced on the ground, possibly incorporating an earlier Iron Age feature. There is also the suggestion of a smaller annexe, and the alignment of both may have changed early in the site's history.

Within this enclosure, which had subdivisions, we might expect to find the buildings described by Adomnán: the church with an attached chamber; a number of working- or sleeping-huts for the monks; Columba's sleeping-hut; a hut 'built in a higher place' and used by him for writing; a house or houses where guests were accommodated; and a communal building, probably containing a kitchen and refectory. The existence of a smithy is also implied. The original church is thought to lie in the vicinity of the medieval abbey, and probably consisted of a timber predecessor to the surviving later stone chapel traditionally known as 'St Columba's Shrine'. Adomnán describes the use of oak timbers and wattle for buildings, and excavations have recovered the remains of circular or oval buildings and a probable rectangular building which was constructed either with sill beams or vertically set planking.

As in Irish monasteries, activities appear to have been zoned, whether for industrial activities (fine-metalworking, leatherworking and woodworking took place at Iona) or to define levels of sanctity. The most important burials took place around the church, but there was also a major cemetery at Reilig Odhráin (used for royal burial) where the second largest collection of early Christian funerary monuments in the British Isles, after Clonmacnois in

55 *Iona, general view.*

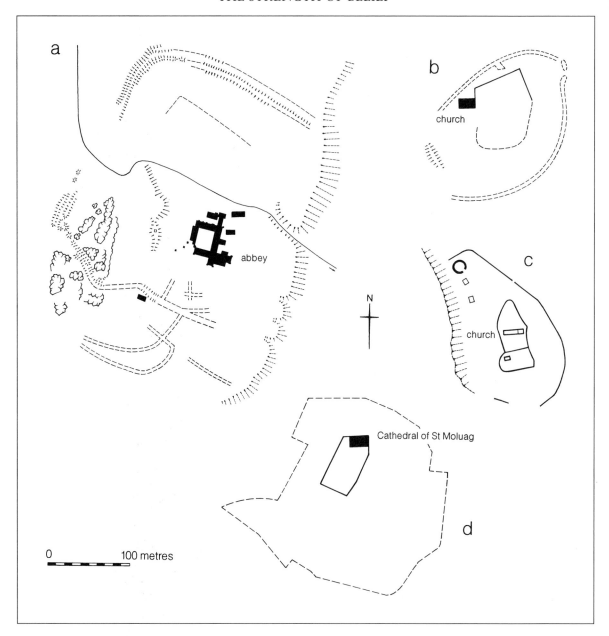

**56** *Comparative plans of* (a) *Iona;* (b) *Applecross;* (c) *Kingarth;* (d) *Lismore (literally 'great enclosure'). There are no remains of early Christian character at Lismore, although field boundaries may perpetuate the line of the vallum.*

Ireland, has been found. There may also have been several other chapels.

Crosses were used to mark burials, define areas of sanctity and as preaching posts. A group of three splendid high crosses, spanning the mid- to late eighth century, were located near the central church and a further high cross may have also marked a probable entrance to the monastery by Reilig Odhráin. Their form and style owe much to the cultural and intellectual interaction between Iona, Pictland, Ireland and Northumbria (57).

Beyond the monastery, Adomnán describes more than one barn and a shed, fields and trackways, where the monks practised a mixed farming economy. Grain was undoubtedly ground at a horizontal water-mill (yet to be found), the large millstones from which were already being used as a cross-base in Adomnán's time. Iona was therefore a largely self-sufficient community, but with access to distant resources (such as building timbers or stone for carving). Although not directly involved in overseas trade, she acquired exotica from the local power centres.

By the time of Adomnán (late seventh century) the monastery was at the peak of its power. Its abbot was effectively a bishop, the head of a monastic confederacy spanning both sides of the North Channel, all subject to the mother house. But there were also large non-Columban monasteries in Scotland: Lismore, founded by St Moluag (see **56d**); several monasteries were founded by the great navigator, St Brendan of Clonfert; Donnán of Eigg made an attempt to evangelize the north-west; from Bangor (Co. Down), Maelrubai followed on his successes in this area and established Applecross (673) (see **56b**); and further south, Kingarth (Bute) was founded by a sixth-century native of the island, St Blane (see **56c**). The term 'Columban Church' is not without drawbacks since it plays down the unsung role of these less well-documented saints, but the alternative 'Celtic Church' is an unhelpful concept, since it implies uniformity throughout Celtic parts of Europe, which was certainly not the case.

Recognition of early Christian sites in general is dependent on: place-names; the size and shape of the enclosure; or the presence of early carvings/early burials/early church buildings/a well. *Cill-, Kil-* (from Latin *cella*, chapel) or *annait* names most probably belong to the period *c.* 500–900 and, especially when combined with the name of an early saint, imply an early foundation. This equation becomes more complicated for those saints who had a long popularity or were the subject of later cults. Chapels cannot always be dated on the basis of field remains alone, but an early date can be

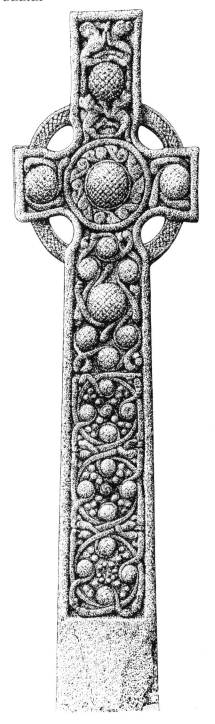

**57** *St Martin's cross, Iona, east face (4.3m/14ft high). Stylistically this relates to St John's and St Oran's crosses (Iona) and the Kildalton cross (Islay) (see **58**). Slots cut into the ends of the arms may have been used to hold applied decorative metalwork (RCAHMS).*

58 *Kildalton cross, east face (2.65m/8½ft high). At the top of the shaft sits the Virgin and Child with angels, while around the hollow central boss (defined by animals) are scenes from the Old Testament: Cain murdering Abel; David killing the lion; and the sacrifice of Isaac by Abraham (RCAHMS).*

suggested when they are associated with circular enclosures and/or early carvings. In the case of Kildalton (Islay), the spectacular late eighth-century cross is, on its own, sufficient grounds for arguing that there must have been a

monastery here, despite the fact that there is no evidence for this on the ground (58). Circular enclosures, perhaps reused settlements, may have been used for burial (and are likely to have been some of the earliest Christian monuments), as in Ireland. The apparent absence of internal structures (as for example at Cill-an-Suidhe, Lismore; 59c) may be due to their timber construction. Recognition of Christian burials (extended inhumations) is not always easy. These are difficult to date due to the lack of grave-goods, and burial orientation is unfortunately not always a reliable guide. Continuity from pagan to Christian sites appears common: a surprising number of sites are associated with wells, which are said to have healing properties; earlier burials precede some chapels (as at St Ninian's Point, Bute, which overlies north-south oriented burials); and place-names such as Cladh a'Bhile, 'burial ground of the sacred tree', recall pagan beliefs and practices. The sanctification of prehistoric monuments by the addition of at least a cross has also been noted at a small number of sites.

In terms of field remains, we can then recognize a range of early Christian sites: lesser religious communities, eremitic sites, caves, chapels, preaching stations and burial grounds. Large enclosures, such as at Cladh a'Bhearnaig (see 59b) or Ardnadam (Cowal) may have been small monasteries. For those preferring more austere life-styles, there were Ceann a'Mhara (see 59a), Eileach an Naoimh (founded by St Brendan of Clonfert in the Garvellachs) (60, 61) or Sgòr nam Ban-Naomha (62). Remote promontory or stack sites in northern Scotland may have fulfilled a similar role. Caves containing early Christian carvings, such as King's Cave (Arran) or Scoor (Mull) may have been the retreats of individuals which subsequently became places of pilgrimage.

We need to know more about the nature of the relationship between the Columban Church in Scotland and the laity if we are to understand how Christianity affected early historic society. If

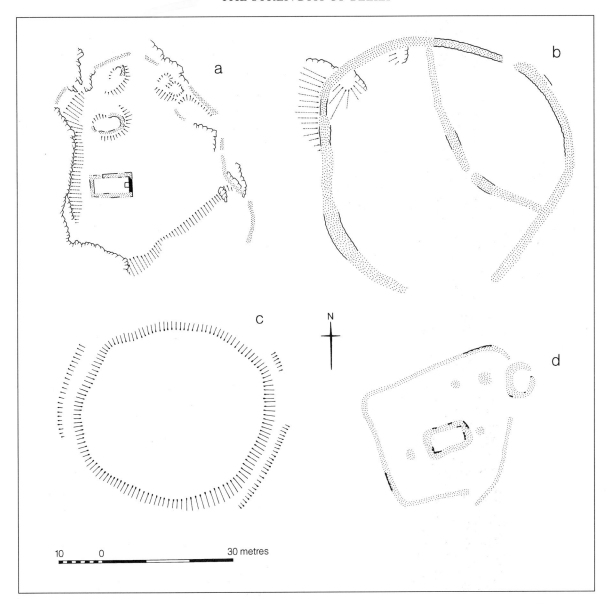

10    0            30 metres

**59** *Comparative plans of lesser early Christian sites: (a) Ceann a'Mhara, Tiree; (b) Cladh a'Bhearnaig, Kerrera; (c) Cill-an-Suidhe, Lismore; (d) Cill Chaitrìona, Colonsay.*

we look to Ireland, then we see that the monasteries effectively formed separate tribes which coexisted alongside their secular equivalents, their leaders sharing the same interests. Abbacies were often hereditary and it was common for one branch of a ruling family to hold the kingship while another controlled the abbacy. We know that the Ionan abbacy tended to stay with Columba's kin and that he was closely involved in secular politics. Kings not only visited him, but he perhaps ordained one of them, Áedán mac Gabhráin, and accompanied him the following

year to Druim Cett (Co. Derry) where a meeting had been convened to sort out a dispute between the Scottish and Irish Dál Riata. We find Adomnán playing a similarly high-profile role in 697 when he negotiated acceptance of his *Law of Innocents* by the kings of Ireland, Argyll and Pictland at the synod of Birr (Co. Offaly). This ecclesiastical law was designed to

60 *Reconstruction of the monastery of Eileach an Naoimh, Garvellachs.*

61 *Beehive cell at Eileach an Naoimh (RCAHMS).*

protect non-combatants (women, children and clergy) from the horrors of war, and it is an indication of his status that he was able to do this.

The picture becomes more complicated when we turn to the role of the clergy in relation to the population at large. In Ireland and Wales it is apparent that the distinction between cloistered monks who lived enclosed lives according to a rule and secular clergy who provided pastoral care to the wider community is blurred, and not helped by the terminology we use. The Irish Church was also under pressure from the laity to provide more pastoral care. Although there were some Dál Riata religious communities who followed ascetic principles, most monasteries would probably have included a range of secular clergy. The larger monasteries would have had claims over a region and its community with regard to their pastoral duties. Adomnán may not specifically mention such work because he took it for granted. On the contrary, King Oswald of Northumbria asked Iona:

> to send a bishop by whose teaching and ministry the English people over whom he ruled might receive the blessings of the Christian Faith and the sacraments ... Henceforward many Irish arrived day by day in Britain and proclaimed the word of God with great devotion ... while those of them who were in priest's orders ministered the grace of baptism to those who believed. Churches were built ... and the people flocked gladly to hear the word of God (Bede, *History* III, 3).

There is therefore no reason why the Columban monks were not also ministering to the Dál Riata. Indeed the laity did come on pilgrimages to the monasteries and hermitages where they provided a source of wealth for the Church.

Penitents were already arriving on Iona in the time of Columba. Although the churches were too small to receive large congregations, the sculpted stones and free-standing crosses or open-air altars (*leachta*) provided stations from which preaching, in the vernacular language, could take place or prayers might be offered. They also came to show respect for individual saints whose remains were sometimes widely distributed in the form of relics. These might be housed in altars (as at St Ninian's Point, Bute), specially marked graves, ornate stone shrines, or portable reliquaries, like the eighth-century house-shaped Monymusk reliquary (**colour plate 11**). Relics such as these would have been used publicly in a range of religious rituals; in a time of drought during Adomnán's time at Iona the relics of Columba were taken in a procession to the 'hill of angels'.

**62** *Sgòr nam Ban-Naomha, Canna. A sophisticated water-supply system may imply that some of the buildings were bath-houses (RCAHMS).*

**63** *Detail of monks on a cross-slab (in St Vigeans Museum).*

In general, however, the clergy may have come to the laity certainly to preach but perhaps also to administer to them at times of baptism, Communion and death. These itinerant clergy travelled with the tools of their trade: Bible, psalter or prayer book (probably in a leather satchel) (**63**); crosier (St Moluag's crosier survives at Lismore); handbell; and perhaps a portable altar. Saint's relics were taken around to enforce the law, to 'validate' the collection of tax or invoke favour from God.

These men perhaps travelled between their religious communities and dependent outstations. Such a relationship has been suggested for the island monastery of Eilean Mór and the Keills cross on the nearby mainland. The distribution of chapels and burial grounds suggests that pastoral care may have been extensive, but there are obviously problems in recognizing how early these might be. One can only speculate as to whether some of the clerics lived with the populace as tenants of the Church rather than in religious communities (clergy were permitted to marry at this time). There is no direct evidence for their role in baptism, although sites such as Cill Chaitrìona (Colonsay) have basins which might have been used for this purpose, and there are of course the holy wells. The role of the Church in burial is also problematic. In Ireland people were buried within enclosures from at least the seventh century, but this did not become the norm until the eighth or ninth century when burial near the bones of saints became a substitute for burial in pagan cemeteries near the bones of ancestors. When did religious pressure for burial in recognized places begin? In the absence of excavation, it is impossible to confirm whether burial grounds contained women and children, and were therefore used by the laity. The picture is complicated by the Christian reuse of some pagan burial grounds, although the earlier burials can be distinguished as they are not oriented east–west. From an early date kings and nobles, on the other hand, appear to have acquired the right to be buried in or near to churches.

Presumably the Church acquired land for its chapels, monasteries, farming and dues by donation and/or in return for prayers. The fate of the monk St Donnán, killed in 617 by Picts on Eigg, however, demonstrates that its presence was not always welcomed.

The role of women in the Church is not known, although place-names such as Sgòr nam Ban-Naomha (Crag of the Holy Women) perhaps imply that they did form their own religious communities, as in Ireland.

## The Columban Church in Pictland

While there is no evidence that Columba himself made widespread conversions outside Loairn, Bede claimed in 731 that Iona had long ruled over the monasteries of the Picts. Evidence to substantiate this largely consists of 14 quadrangular iron bells, dedications to early saints and cross-marked boulders and pillar stones (64). Adomnán stated that there were monasteries in Pictland in his time and the inference must be that within about fifty years of Columba's death his followers, and perhaps those of other pioneering missionaries, may have been organizing an infant Church centred on the Moray Firth. The difficulty is in distinguishing evidence for this from the later influences of the Columban Church, reintroduced by the mac Ailpín dynasty after a period in which the Roman Church had dominated (see below). Seven bronze handbells (c. 900) belong to this later phase, but some of the iron handbells can possibly be attributed to the earlier Church. Their distribution argues for the direct intervention of Columba's followers in southern Pictland.

Simple cross-incised stones (Class IV) bear no other ornament, and are hence difficult to date,

but some of these are likely to pre-date sculpture combining Christian iconography and Pictish symbols. Evidence for this type of monument is still very much at the data-collection stage, but there is hope that an early Columban strata related to the seventh-century activities of Columba's followers could perhaps be traced. Comparison of the distribution in Argyll of crosses with expanded terminals (found on a quern at Dunadd, and various known early Christian foundations) with the distribution of all other types of crosses demonstrates that this particular form was restricted to areas where early monks from Iona are known to have been active; hopefully similar successful observations could be made in Pictland.

So while there were obviously some Christians and Christian communities in seventh-century Pictland – indeed it has been argued that Christianity was quite well known in southern Pictland by 600 – we do not know the extent of the Church's influence on society. Only the royal foundation of Abernethy, Perthshire, a sometime episcopal centre, *may* have an origin in the seventh century. Otherwise the first evidence that the Church was exerting any significant influence on Pictish society as a whole comes with the activities of King Nechtán from c. 710 when the Roman church was introduced.

## Roman Church

Ostensibly the Roman Church differed from the Columban Church in so far as it was based on territorial dioceses, had a hierarchical structure, and its clergy recognized the authority of bishops and did not follow monastic vows. But it is easy to exaggerate the differences when, as we have seen above, Irish abbots and bishops claimed pastoral jurisdiction over regions and their communities. They would also have been difficult to distinguish in terms of physical remains, especially when priests lived together in centres from which they ministered to dependent churches spread among large parishes.

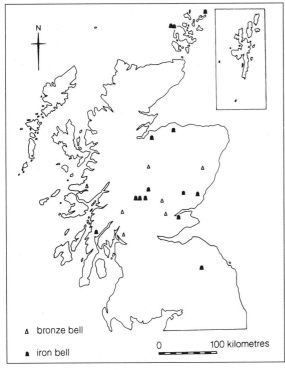

△ bronze bell
▲ iron bell

0    100 kilometres

**64** *Distribution of handbells.*

**65** *North face of a small Anglo-Saxon church at Escomb, Co. Durham. Nechtán's church at* Egglespethir *is likely to have been similar: long rectangular nave connected to small square chancel by tall narrow arch; high, small windows; unornamented; and set within a circular burial ground (B.T. Batsford).*

The Columban Church had been introduced to Northumbria in 634 by Aidan, a monk from Iona, but its tenure was short-lived. A dispute arose with advocates of the Roman Church. Ostensibly about the date of Easter and styles of tonsure, this was in reality a power struggle, a fight by the king for jurisdiction over the church. The matter was resolved in favour of the Roman Church at the synod of Whitby in 664. Back in Argyll, the monks of Iona were deprived of their influence over the Northumbrian Church and reluctant to accept this change: Adomnán was persuaded in 688, but the monks did not follow until 712.

A similar struggle for royal authority lies behind the events of *c.* 710. King Nechtán sent messengers to Abbot Ceolfrith of Monk-wearmouth (Northumbria) seeking advice on changing the Pictish Church from Columban to Roman observance, and for architects to build a church in the Roman style. The prime mover behind Nechtán's action was almost certainly an influential English monk called Egbert, who was also instrumental in persuading the monks of Iona to accept the Roman ways. On receipt of his instructions, Nechtán enforced the Catholic Easter and 'the reformed nation was glad to be

placed under the direction of Peter, the most blessed of the apostles' (Bede, *History* V, 21). His stone church, built at *Egglespethir* near Restenneth, Angus (exact location unknown), was founded by priests *and* monks, and seems to have had an extensive jurisdiction in Pictland (**65**). Subsequently, the *'familia* of Iona', those who had not converted to the Roman ways, were expelled from Pictland.

Why then did Nechtán decide to introduce the Roman Church? Patently a pious king, who ultimately retired to a monastery, the answer is also political. In approaching Northumbria for guidance he was seeking unity with his southern neighbours at a time of political insecurity. The hierarchical organization of the Roman Church tallied well with secular forms of administration. The conscious introduction of this new-style Church was therefore an effective way of both consolidating and extending royal authority, particularly to areas which may still have been ripe for conversion. Land was granted to the Church whose clergy, in tandem with the nobility, acted as the king's local agents and representatives. The local nobles derived additional authority by their association with this fashionable, new source of power which also widened their career opportunities. Its pastoral system was a means of extending and establishing an ideology which was pro-State. The Church was also able to assist in administrative matters (see below). This type of symbiosis between king and Church was a recognized phenomenon throughout north-west Europe in the eighth century. In return, the Church obtained the land (and associated rights) which it needed both to survive and to generate wealth for its own works. Ecclesiastics were in effect ideologically endowed nobility who derived their authority from their access to Christianity.

Nechtán's reforms were effective and extended as far as the Northern Isles. As Class I stones indicate, Orkney was already part of the Pictish orbit in the seventh century, but the establishment of the Roman Church marks its absorption into the Pictish kingdom and perhaps the extension of authority to Shetland. There are legends of a person called St Boniface building 150 churches in Pictland. Clearly this was not the better-known Devonian saint of the same name who led a famous mission to central Germany. However, the monk Egbert may have been involved in the organization of both missions, which could explain similarities between the two. There are Scottish traditions of someone called Boniface and someone called Curetan, but these are obviously conflated and appear therefore to refer to the same person. It appears that Curetan was instrumental in the introduction of the Roman Church to the north and subsequently changed his name to Boniface to mark allegiance to Roman practices.

An even geographical distribution of definite and possible dedications to St Peter in Orkney, each referred to as a kirk rather than a chapel, grander than might have been expected, and sited on the top of broch mounds (high-status prehistoric sites likely to have been gifted by secular rulers) can be identified. According to legend, St Tredwell, a holy virgin, accompanied Boniface on his mission to the Picts. Dedications on Papa Westray to them both, suggest that a Northern Isles bishopric may have been intended for here, at a central location. The Norse place-name *papa* (monks), found throughout the Northern Isles, is more likely to represent pastoral clergy than eremites, given their juxtaposition with fertile land where the laity would have lived. The fact that the Norse specifically referred to the monks is also an indication of their significance in the local political geography.

Boniface is also credited with building a church at Rosemarkie, from where his Orcadian mission may have been monitored. The large collection of carved stones from here and other sites around the Moray Firth (Shandwick, Tarbat, Hilton of Cadboll and Nigg) testifies to the presence of a vigorous and wealthy Church in this area.

So, to what extent was the pastoral element of the Roman Church any greater, in practice, than in the Columban Church? Obviously this was a primary function for its clergy, and their success can best be measured in the Class II stones (**66, 67**), which are found throughout

**66** *Example of a Class II stone at Migvie (Tom Gray).*

**67** *Jet pendant in Inverness Museum, a Class II stone in portable form? (front and back).*

**68** *Distribution of select types of early historic sculpted stones (those without Pictish symbols). Many of the cross-slabs fragments may have formed part of monuments which did originally include symbols.*

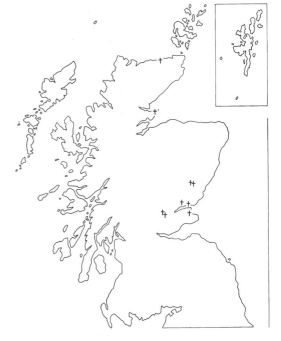

+ free-standing cross (Pictland)

0    100 kilometres

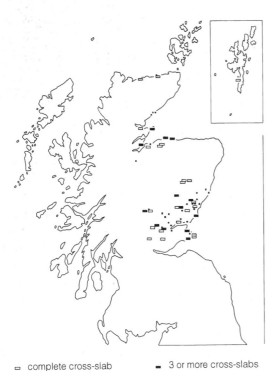

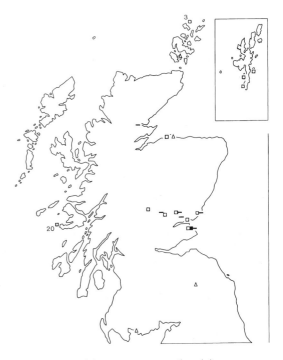

&#9633; complete cross-slab   &#9644; 3 or more cross-slabs

&#9642; cross-slab fragment

&#9633; corner-post shrine   &#9651; other shrine

&#9642; solid shrine    &#9644; recumbent slab

Pictland. The greatest preponderance of these lies to the south of the Mounth, possibly because Nechtán's mission was strongest closest to home, or because there were already believers in this area (see above). Either way, it appears that the local aristocracy gave the Church its full support. Most of these and subsequent Christian carvings (sometimes called Class III, i.e. without Pictish symbols, but otherwise a meaningless classification since this technically encompasses a very wide range of monuments) are found at or nearby the sites of later medieval parish churches or burial grounds, suggesting that these were centres of Christian worship and/or burial from the eighth century, if not before (**68**). The Class II stones were not used to mark individual burials, but were public statements about the beliefs of the wider community and the taste and sophistication of their patrons. We might expect to find them near the *caput* of a thanage and at each estate centre, with or without an associated (timber) church or burial ground.

Many of the Class II slabs were probably erected in the years following Nechtán's approach to Northumbria. Their form and the adoption of interlace are an imaginative and distinctive response by Pictish masons to the artistic and technological inspiration of their Northumbrian counterparts, a legacy of the close relationship between the two kingdoms (**69**). More importantly, their content encapsulates the changing political scene. On one side of them can be found a magnificent cross, glorifying God. The reverse is usually reserved for images of the secular patrons (usually male), whose status is reinforced by their depiction in the noble pursuits of hunting and riding. Only on the stone from Hilton of Cadboll (now in Edinburgh) do we find an image of a female patron depicted in the familiar hunting scene (in this instance accompanied by trumpeters) (**70**). Many of these images had both secular and religious meaning. Hunting scenes might allude to the Christian soul in pursuit of Christ (the deer) and salvation. Other images were

**69** *Cross-slab at Aberlemno churchyard.*

more explicit references to Bible stories, although some mythological themes might also have been appropriated for Christian purposes. These are juxtaposed with revamped Pictish designs whose relevance is obviously transferable to a Christian context. Although in future these would be omitted from Christian carvings, in these first years of the new Church it was still considered appropriate and/or necessary to include them.

We will never know if the imagery, particularly the decision to depict the nobles, was selected (in deference?) by the Church or demanded by its secular patrons. Either way,

these monuments were very clever pieces of propaganda, testimonies to the rights of the Church to the land and confirmation of its jurisdiction. The use of designs can be understood at several levels. Firstly the designs evoke both the status and ritual authority of the secular patrons, aspects of which they have now passed to the Church. Yet at the same time the designs are being employed in a familiar 'votive' context – invoking Godly favours – and their message would still be understood by a wider public. At a third level, they consciously refer to the sense of Pictish identity, an identity already promoted on Class I stones. But this is now a deliberate attempt to relate this familiar, comprehensively

70 *Hunting scene on the stone found at Hilton of Cadboll (NMS).*

71 *Hunting scene on one of the stones beside the road in Aberlemno.*

recognized symbolism to a new, politically motivated, ideology, which radiates from southern Pictland, having appropriated symbolism most closely associated with the north-east (hence Class II stones develop later in this area).

Nowhere in Argyll do we find such blatant evidence for the association of the Church with its secular peers, as the sculpture of the two areas makes clear. There are no obvious early depictions of secular lords nor are there, with one or two exceptions, any images of clerics. Contrast this with Pictland where Class II sculptures include prominent images of at least one of these social groups (**71**). There was patently an increasing involvement between the Pictish Church and lay people, as can be seen in the foundation of religious houses, often within close proximity of the secular power centres. Some of these developed into major ecclesiastical centres, to judge from the large collections of carvings which have been found. At Meigle, Perthshire, architectural fragments also suggest a stone structure of some kind, although not necessarily a church (**72**). Many of the carvings are now new types of burial monuments (e.g. recumbent slabs) and they demonstrate that the Church has firmly established its role with regard to the burial of the nobility, if not other laity. Abernethy, if not already founded (see above), was established close to the fort at Clatchard Craig. The enthusiasm and initiative which kings and nobles took in establishing these religious foundations suggest that the Church also fulfilled a supplementary role to secular administration, not least through its access to the technology of writing.

## The use of writing

We have already examined the evidence for the lack of surviving early historic written sources (Chapter 2), but how prevalent was literacy, how and when was it used?

Literacy was promoted by the Church: in Ireland Patrick issued his monks and new converts with the rudiments of knowledge, which

**72** *Wide collection of sculpted stones as displayed in Meigle in 1953. Includes recumbent slabs, some with slots for uprights or perhaps relics (RCAHMS).*

may have included alphabets. Alphabet stones, known from both Ireland and Scotland (**73**), may have been teaching aids but are more likely to have been symbolic statements about access to literacy and the Word of God. The ability to read and write, and/or access to someone who could do this, was the passport to enlightenment. Leading members of the Church, such as Adomnán and Columba, were clearly well-travelled, highly educated, literate people, conversant with current ideology and intellectual trends in north-west Europe; the complex iconography of ecclesiastical art confirms that neither the Columban nor Roman Church was in any way intellectually handicapped. Indeed, the library of Iona contained

books on Near Eastern topography. Adomnán took his own notes on wax tablets which he or his fellow monks could copy on to expensive vellum in the scriptorium from which, in due course, came the *Book of Kells*. Given that Iona was such a literate community, the small number of stone inscriptions may be surprising. Other monasteries too had the capacity to produce ornate, illuminated texts; surviving metalwork and stone-carving of this period certainly imply an active and widespread manuscript tradition. The rare survival of a carved Latin text from Tarbat (see **10**) implies that this monastery had the capacity to produce books in an accomplished Insular script. Foreign models in the form of manuscripts and perhaps textiles must have also been widely circulated, to judge from the Northumbrian, continental and Byzantine influences which are prevalent in the artwork (**74**).

**73** *Alphabet stone at Lochgoilhead: sequences of letters in alphabetic order (RCAHMS).*

**74** *A carving from Riasg Buidhe, Colonsay, with its closest parallels in Ireland where the source of inspiration was Mediterranean art. In Celtic iconography the 'decapitated' head is sometimes regarded as a phallic symbol. However, the blatant phallic nature of the reverse of this carving (not shown) is unusual (RCAHMS).*

Being literate gave people the ability to accumulate knowledge about the past and the natural world, to store texts through time and to transmit them over greater distances. Social relations could be extended *beyond* face-to-face transactions. In the case of the Church, there was therefore the capacity to authorize new religious beliefs while fulfilling and developing its own intellectual and religious needs. It did so through study of the Scriptures and other holy writings, use of texts in its religious observance, compilation and circulation of saints' *Lives*, erection of dedications and memorials, and the creation of laws (such as Adomnán's *Law of Innocents*, see above).

King Alfred of Wessex tried to make his subjects more literate so that they could familiarize themselves with the Word of God, but literacy remained virtually a clerical monopoly in Saxon England too. Kings and nobles were probably the only lay people who acquired writing and reading skills; Northumbrian kings trained at Iona, and it is possible that, as in Ireland, Pictish and Dál Riata nobles also received some schooling. More mundane objects with ogham suggest that some of the laity had access to writing. The presence of yellow manuscript pigment and a stone disc with a Christian inscription at Dunadd confirm that there could be literate people at power centres, but the majority of writing probably took place at monastic scriptoria, which were often located nearby.

The question then is, to what extent did kings use writing in government? Clearly from as early as the late seventh-century documents, such as *Senchus fer nAlban* (see Chapter 2), were produced in order to legitimize and authorize claims to secular power and position. Genealogies, regnal lists and possibly the annals would have fulfilled a similar function. Writing was therefore exploited as soon as the higher echelons of society accepted Christianity. King Nechtán made good use of it: he corresponded with Bishop Ceolfrith of Northumbria about the Roman Church and sent new Easter cycles 'throughout all the Provinces of the Picts to be transcribed, learned and observed' (Bede, *History* V, 21). He and his more learned men apparently understood Latin. We have no proof that he also corresponded with his secular followers, or indeed they with him, but it seems unavoidable with the increasing distances over which he needed to operate. In particular, we would have expected land grants to be recorded. In addition, we might also anticipate

that there was a greater reliance on written 'rules' or laws but, whether or not these were ever committed to vellum, it would still have been their verbal oration which gave them the force of law.

## The later Church

Throughout north-west Europe the idea of the reborn Christian Roman empire became popular after *c.* 750 – mirrored in the series of Pictish kings called Constantín (Constantine) – and the developing relationship between the Church and State can be seen in the flowering of officially sponsored ecclesiastical art. The splendid St Andrews sarcophagus, discovered in 1833 in the precincts of the later cathedral, was probably first erected within a royal chapel or monastic church, where it possibly commemorated Óengus mac Fergusa (died 761) (**colour plate 12**).

Pictish designs are not found on eighth-century silver metalwork and around this time they also ceased to be used on ecclesiastical sculpture, whether on dressed slabs or later free-standing crosses (a new form of monument found also in Argyll). The content of sculptures also changed: instead of hunting scenes, the secular authorities tended to be depicted in a militaristic stance, as on the ninth-century Dupplin cross. Erected only a few miles away from the royal palace of Forteviot, on the opposite bank of the River Earn, we see here a king on horseback (**75**), possibly identified from an inscription now recognized on an upper panel of the cross as Constantín mac Fergusa (*c.* 789–820) (**76**). Beneath and around him are several ranks of foot-soldiers: men with moustaches and ornamented hems on their tunics, and younger men with neither. A similar cross apparently originally overlooked Forteviot from Invermay, on the opposite side of the Strath. Clearly the abandonment of Pictish designs on such monuments marks a significant political development, but what? The militaristic stance of the soldiers at Dupplin

*75 Dupplin cross; the 'empty' upper panel on the west face is now recognized to contain an inscription (2.6m/8½ft high) (Allen and Anderson; Society of Antiquaries of Scotland).*

*76 Dupplin cross, cast of inscription: CU [...] NTIN/ FILIUSFIRCU/S (NMS).*

provides clues, since it suggests a strengthening and formalization of royal authority. At least that is the image which the kings wished to be understood by the people who encountered them. As such the symbolism of the Pictish designs has become redundant: these monuments are proclaiming a positive future, in the secure arms of the Church, rather than seeking legitimization in pagan symbols of former status and glory. Additionally, the highly charged Pictishness of the designs would have run counter to the new interests of the Gaelic kings.

Constantín mac Fergusa is sometimes credited with the foundation of a major new ecclesiastical foundation at Dunkeld, perhaps

*77 Crieff mounts; later reused as horse furniture, these could have been from a decorated altar, reliquary or cross, and were perhaps part of a relic brought from Iona by Cináed mac Ailpín (NMS).*

(77). We can but imagine the spectacle of popular devotion which would have accompanied their formal translation. Cináed and his descendants favoured the post-Columban Church, now revitalized in Pictland by new monastic foundations, although revised Church organization may have emphasized episcopal authority.

In this Chapter we have seen how both the Columban and Roman Churches were introduced. They gained their power, like secular lords, from access to land and associated rights which was granted to them. Many establishments were very wealthy and in reaction to their worldliness and secularization the eighth/ninth-century Céli Dé (Servants of God) movement attempted to introduce reforms. In addition to providing administrative support for the king and nobility, the Church advocated an ideology which was pro-State and hence supported the aspirations of kings, who now modelled themselves upon leaders of the former Christian Roman empire. The influence of the Church permeated all levels of society and was probably the most successful and effective method by which the authority of kings could be peacefully extended. It did so by extolling a belief system which not only transcended the bonds of social relations linked to agricultural production, but also by overseeing this in its capacity as a major landowner. Through it we can trace evidence for the consolidation of society. But before discussing when this effectively took place, we must turn to examine the fourth source of power – military might.

at the time of the abandonment of Iona in the early ninth century. But it was Cináed mac Ailpín in 849 who affirmed its status by bringing to it some of the relics of St Columba (split with the monastery of Kells after Viking raids finally forced the monks to leave Iona), hence dividing spiritual authority. It is an indication of Cináed's authority that he was able to acquire these prestigious, venerated objects

# CHAPTER SIX

# From 'wandering thieves' to lords of war

Not only is the early historic period throughout the British Isles characterized by the emergence of warlike, heroic kings who ruled over defined territories, but we can also detect certain changes in the nature and circumstances of combat. This changing face of military aggression encapsulates many of the political, social and religious developments of the period, most of which have already been referred to in the preceding Chapters.

Warfare was a major and regular component of early historic life. Heroic literature, such as the *Gododdin*, paints a picture of an aggressive society in which petty kings and their personal warrior retinues were 'nurtured on wine and mead' and fought to obtain personal glory and material wealth. Contemporary poetry was used to reinforce heroic concepts of behaviour. Many of their campaigns, which followed a ritualistic formula, may simply have been to plunder or exact tribute, rather than in pursuance or defence of territorial ambitions. Acquisition of slaves may have been an additional motive. Slave-trading was common in the Roman period (if not before): Patrick (later a saint), kidnapped from near Carlisle and taken to Ireland, is the best-known victim. Northern British kings also enslaved some of those they conquered, undoubtedly applying them to agricultural production. There was a Dál Riata slave-girl at the Pictish court of Bridei mac Máelchú when Columba visited it. Regardless of the purpose, fighting generally took place

between leaders of different territories, such as kindreds of Dál Riata, or between the different peoples of north Britain. Gildas, admittedly a biased observer, described both the Picts and Dál Riata in the sixth century as 'wandering thieves who had no taste for war' and 'in perfect accord in their greed for bloodshed'. But from the annals we can begin to piece together a different picture where kings sought to both extend and formalize the extent of their territories. Áedán mac Gabhráin is a classic example of a warlord. Overlord of Dál Riata from 574, by land and sea he successfully campaigned against Pictland for many years (as far north as the Orkneys) and against the Angles, until in 603 he was defeated at *Degsastan*, somewhere in Northumbria. Clearly sea-routes and Roman roads were commonly employed to transport large forces over considerable distances.

The inheritance of kingdoms was usually hotly contested by rival kin groups which, due to intermarriage, might also include eligible foreigners. Power centres, which had a defensive capacity (Chapter 3), were targeted for siege, capture and burning, and the terse accounts of these events – for example, '683 Siege of Dundurn' – may be scribal shorthand for shifts in the distribution of authority and peoples associated with these power centres. Certainly, it is hard to imagine that monks would have recorded anything less significant, unless it was simply to catalogue the iniquities of their secular contemporaries for their own, sanctimonious, purposes. However, most combat is likely to have taken place away from the power centres, where the space was available for set-piece battles, whether at sea or on land, both of which are documented.

## Battles at sea

Both the Picts and Dál Riata were known to the Romans as sea-raiders, and they clearly continued to use the seaways for communication, trade and attack. Vegetius, a fourth-century Roman writer, describes camouflaged scout-boats with sails, ropes and twenty rowers which have sometimes been attributed to the Picts, although the evidence is slender. The earliest specific reference to a sea-battle in the British Isles refers to a battle between the Cenél Loairn and Cenél nGabhráin in 719. Yet as early as the 580s Áedán mac Gabhráin was already campaigning in the Orkneys and the Isle of Man. Both the Picts and Dál Riata could clearly muster large navies: 150 Pictish ships were wrecked in 729. Seafare was therefore both a normal and an essential component of

*78 St Orland's stone, Cossans, Angus (Tom Gray).*

life, as testified by Adomnán's reference to at least fifty-five separate journeys in his account of Columba's life. We are also frequently reminded of the perils of the sea: 'Failbe ... the successor of Maelrubai of Applecross, was drowned in the deep sea with his sailors, twenty-two in number.' The Dál Riata would also have been familiar with merchant ships from southern Britain, Gaul and perhaps the Mediterranean, which were bringing imported goods to their shores.

On the basis of Adomnán's descriptions, some of the Dál Riata ships could be large (carrying over twenty people) and, while all used oars, the largest could be fitted with a mast and sail. Some may have been navigated by professional sailors. As to the construction of the boats, the monks of Iona acquired pine and oak for a *longa navis*, ('long ship') but we do not know if any boats were made exclusively of timber. More probably they were skin-covered currachs, a form of construction which, by then, already had a pedigree in Ireland of about 4000 years.

Far less is known about Pictish boats. In general these too may have been skin-covered, although the double-ended, mastless rowing-boat illustrated on the stone at St Orland's, may have been wooden (**78**), as may have been the boat carved on the cave wall at Jonathan's Cave, East Weemys.

## Battles on land

When it comes to the nature of fighting on land, we know almost as little. There are no detailed accounts to match the account provided by Tacitus of Agricola's victory over the Britons at Mons Graupius in 83. Here the allied forces of the British tribes included chariots and foot-soldiers (who fought with huge swords for slashing and carried small shields). The *Gododdin* gives little away about early historic battle tactics or weapon-handling and few weapons themselves survive (unlike in neighbouring Bernicia, where pagan warriors were buried with them). The

79 *Cross-slab from Benvie (Tom Gray).*

sculpted stones provide greater detail, with their depictions of spears, axes, decorated shields (both square and round) and swords (**79**; see **2**). Crossbows, as shown on a number of sculptures, were probably only used in hunting. Only the St Ninian's Isle chape and sword pommel (**80**, see **colour plate 7**) and possible silver shield-covering from the Norrie's Law hoard demonstrate that the Picts did possess some embellished weaponry. The last reference to the use of chariots was in the early third century, but carefully bred horses are likely to have been an essential component of warfare: for transport to and from battle, for the military posturing which undoubtedly preceded action, and for battle itself. The majority of soldiers probably fought on foot with battle on horseback limited

to kings and nobles, as illustrated on the carvings on the cross-slab at Aberlemno churchyard (**81**). On the reverse of this cross-slab is a battle scene, interpreted as a cartoon-style account of the battle of *Nechtanesmere*, which took place about 10km (6 miles) away in 685. There is likely to have been a religious foundation here at Aberlemno, to judge from the number of stones which have been found in its vicinity. This stone was surely erected under royal stimulus (perhaps Óengus mac Fergusa) to make a political statement about Pictish independence. It unites the worship of Christianity with the recital of royal history, a history which revels in both the hierarchical nature of society and royal achievements (political and religious) obtained by military or other means. It is therefore slightly ironic that the design of the cross (on the opposite side of the Aberlemno churchyard stone) should have owed so much to Northumbrian sources of inspiration.

The aim of much of this aggression was first to acquire a given area, and then to assert authority, perhaps extending it to neighbouring

80 *Inscribed sword chape from the St Ninian's Isle treasure. It reads (upside down) 'Property of son of holy spirit' and on the opposite side 'In name of God' (NMS).*

**81** *Reverse of the cross-slab at Aberlemno churchyard (see 69). In this battle scene the Anglian king Ecgfrith is distinguished from the Picts by his helmet, similar to the one found at Coppergate, York in 1982. From top to bottom: Ecgfrith flees from Bridei, dropping his sword and shield; Ecgfrith is opposed by foot-soldiers, defended with shields, lance and spear; Bridei and Ecgfrith oppose each other in battle; Ecgfrith is killed (symbolized by the raven eating his corpse).*

territories. In pursuit of this ambition, highly mobile armies and navies covered considerable distances. The loyalty and/or submission of the local leaders was paramount, by their death if need be. If not on the battlefield, this might take the form of drowning, a ritual practice with its origins in Gaul. The Pictish kings are recorded

drowning enemy leaders in 734 and 739. Decapitation may also have been practised, as depicted on Sueno's stone, near Forres (**82**). Irish sources refer on several occasions to the tradition of using heads as trophies of war and the human head had been deeply symbolic since the Iron Age throughout Celtic Europe. Decapitation is a practice which anthropologists tend to ascribe to societies with weak military organization, although the available evidence suggests this was not necessarily the case in later Pictland or Argyll (indeed, the Romans followed the same practice); perhaps we are seeing on Sueno's stone a conscious allusion to traditions of much earlier fighting practices.

To ensure that these redefined political relationships were maintained and upheld by the regular submission of tribute, high-status hostages were often taken by the victors and presumably detained at power centres. It was also traditional for kings to transfer the upbringing of their children to foster-parents in different lineages, the intention being that concerns about the safety of their children would deter aggression, although this ploy did not always succeed.

One of the key points to note is how such shifts in authority revolved around the personal ambitions of key individuals – the kings and territorial lords – and how unstable and short-lived any political liaisons might actually be. However a king died – whether violently or in his bed – there was always enormous competition among rivals to be his successor.

## Organization for war

We have yet to consider the contribution which military might made to the extension and consolidation of Argyll, Pictland and their political union. Clearly the ultimate success of any one individual or group was not simply the incremental product of *ad hoc* military ventures. On the contrary, in both Argyll and Pictland we find evidence that kings were placing an increasing emphasis on organizing themselves for war. There was a shift from plundering, pillaging and extortion to pitched battles which required far greater military organization and resources. For example, enormous efforts went in to the breeding and stabling of horses, and the groom, seen accompanying the female on the Hilton of Cadboll stone (see **70**), must have been an important member of the royal household. Indeed, as stone-carvings testify, society was increasingly hierarchical and specialized posts were undoubtedly a natural consequence of this. Further resources must also have been required to free warriors for either permanent or temporary duty. The kings were able to do this because of the existence of sophisticated mechanisms for the exploitation of the agricultural produce of the land (Chapter 4). Similar mechanisms also existed for mustering and equipping both the army and navy.

The *Senchus fer nAlban* was compiled in the late seventh century to inform an overking how much tribute could be expected from the Dál Riata. The number of households within each kindred is itemized, as is the number of men and ships each household should provide for military expeditions: each 20 houses were required to provide 2 seven-benched ships for a sea expedition, for example. It is therefore estimated that Argyll could have raised an army of about 2000 men, or the equivalent of 140 seven-benched ships. Similar arrangements may have existed in Pictland where the predecessors of *mormaer* – territorial magnates – are likely to have exercised military duties as well as fulfilling a fiscal role. Their duties may therefore have extended to mustering and training a quota of young men from the estates under their authority.

By the late eighth century there had also been a change in the perception of how kings viewed themselves, including their military role. This transformation relates largely to the influence of the Church, which was behind a school of thought which wanted to change the character and succession practices of kingship. It wished to create a more peaceful society in

82 *Sueno's stone, east face.*

which a king was inviolate, ruled peacefully, and where there was an orderly and legitimate form of succession upon his death, rather than bloodshed and feud. This school of thought, championed by Adomnán among others, was pervasive and influential throughout Europe, as can be seen in the sculpture of Pictland and, to a lesser extent Argyll, with their David iconography (see **17**, **58**, **75** and **colour plate 12**). The content of the sculpture also changed (Chapter 5): instead of hunting scenes, the secular authorities tended to be depicted in a militaristic stance, as on the Dupplin cross or Sueno's stone. The new imagery suggests a strengthening and formalization of royal authority and we may also find here an explicit reference to an increasingly professional, perhaps full-time, body of soldiers. Given the heroic nature of early historic society, the absence of physical depictions of warriors from earlier sculpture is marked but can be better understood in the context of the Pictish symbols, which would appear to signify, through abstract symbolism, the status and heroic qualities of individuals or groups of people (Chapter 5).

Military aggression can therefore be seen as a continual undercurrent throughout the period. It could be - indeed frequently was - used to decide which particular person inherited or acquired authority over any given area. Kings had to be strong. We must also assume that this was how Cináed mac Ailpín rose to power in Argyll, authority which he was subsequently able to extend to fill a power vacuum in Pictland. Similarly, we know that when Cináed met with local resistance to his takeover, he tackled the problem by military means. So military might was also used to obtain and assert power. Such instances of internecine strife and apparent political instability are recurrent themes throughout this period, and the knee-jerk reaction was to take recourse in further violence.

But kings now needed more than material wealth, personal charisma and military might to stay in effective control of such large areas. They needed the support of the Church. Christianity had led to changes in the character of kingship which go some way to explaining how more permanent structures of government came into place. With the advent of Christianity, kingship was redefined. In theory the Church now interceded on behalf of a king and his people, and clerics began to play a prominent role in inauguration (Chapter 3). They also tried to influence how future kings were chosen, in order to ensure a more stable society, and were pro-State in their ideology (Chapter 5). The Church acknowledged that it could not stop kings fighting, but it could encourage a king to be 'strong like David in crushing his enemies yet lowly in the sight of God' (Eddius Stephanus, *Life of Bishop Wilfrid*). The biblical image of David, the powerful yet holy warrior-king, was exploited throughout contemporary Europe; indeed, David was the Carolingian court's nickname for Emperor Charlemagne. We find tangible acknowledgement of this attitude in Christian invocations on weapons, such as on one of the St Ninian's Isle sword chapes (see **80**) and the content of sculpture, where battle imagery is used to transmit messages of salvation and redemption.

## Warrior saints

Although the Church largely decried violence, some saints, Columba in particular, developed a cult status associated with their power as victory givers. In other words, they fulfilled the role of earlier pagan, warlike deities. Columba came from the warrior aristocracy and patently had an abiding personal interest in battles; he may even have left Ireland in penitence for his involvement in warfare which, among other things, had left him with a 'livid scar' on his side. Despite this, he did not eschew violence when it could be used in the cause of justice, and indeed encouraged it: a penitent was given a sword with which to settle an unjust score before returning to fulfil his life as a monk. Within fifty years of his death, belief in him was thought to secure military victory, and relics associated with him later became employed as talismans in battle. His prayer book, the *Cathac* or 'Battler', was enshrined and used in Ireland by the O'Donnells to secure victory in battle, while his crosier and a house-shaped reliquary were put to similar effect in Scotland (**83**). In later

times the Gaelic-Norse inhabitants of western Scotland were to see him as their protector, attributing to him some of the 'qualities' of the Viking war-god, Odin.

It is difficult to assess the relative contribution of military aggression to the development and consolidation of Pictland and the takeover by Dál Riata kings. Clearly conflict was a major component of early historic society, but this alone cannot account for the political,

**83** *Monymusk reliquary, interior (now empty). This is believed to be the* breacbannach *of St Columba, a talisman used in battle (including Bannockburn in 1314), guarded by a hereditary keeper (see* **colour plate 11***)(NMS).*

social, economic and ideological developments of the times. Yet from out of this *Alba* was born: the final Chapter draws together these strands of evidence to suggest how the Pictish and Dál Riata nations became a political unity.

# CHAPTER SEVEN

# *Alba:* the emergence of the Scottish nation

It is a remarkable achievement that such a geographically extended and diverse group of peoples as the Picts could have been identified as a unity since the late Roman period. Equally extraordinary is the fact that this relationship should have survived the withdrawal of the Romans, the external threat which had first impelled the Iron Age tribes of Scotland to bond in adversity against a common enemy. Over the following centuries this fragile unity was continually buffeted, both internally and externally, by the ebb and flow of power; generations of petty, warrior kings struggled to obtain, maintain and extend their personal authority. Ultimately, however, this loose confederation of Pictish peoples began to consolidate, a process to which their neighbours made a major contribution. Regrettably very little is known of the likely considerable involvement of Strathclyde, but the intimate role of Argyll is better charted, as is the more short-lived, direct involvement of Northumbria. Yet before considering the issue of consolidation between the Picts and Dál Riata, we must first examine the extent to which the Pictish peoples had laid the foundations for this.

## The consolidation of power

In previous Chapters we have explored the various strategies which early historic leaders could use both to create, extend and maintain their authority: overlapping, closely intermeshed strands of military, economic, political and ideological power. The power of kings was highly personalized and informal, resulting in hotly contested competition for the inheritance of territories, the victor usually being the person with the greatest and strongest military backing. But once in power, further means were needed to persuade people to acquiesce to new distributions of authority, as we have seen. Why then did the Pictish peoples begin to consolidate as opposed to confederate; how, where and when did this process take place?

## How?

In order to consolidate power, the Pictish overkings would have needed to effectively strengthen their authority throughout the expanse of Pictland. A model can be suggested for how the four major components of society – the 'State'/highest authorities, Church, political elite and majority of the population – interrelated (84). In general terms, this model is equally applicable to *Alba*.

In this model, leaders extended the distance over which their authority could operate by obtaining the support of the Church and political elite, who effectively acted as their agents in areas beyond where the kings could effectively operate themselves. These were the *mormaer* and thanes, usually the native, local elite whose personal authority had gradually increased as the number of lesser local leaders diminished.

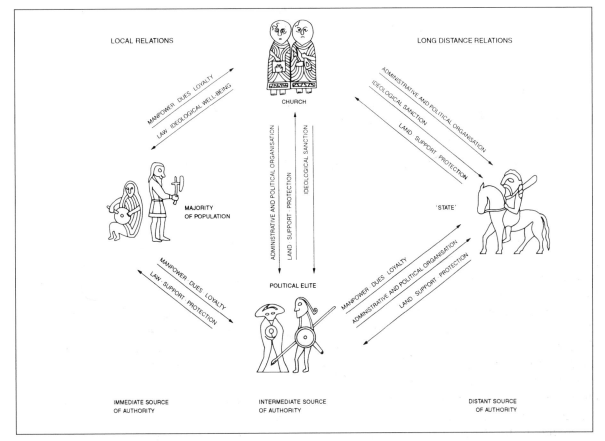

84 *Suggested model for the relationship between resources and the structuring of social authority over time and space.*

Often the *mormaer* were scions of former tribal dynasties who continued to be local kings in all but name, while the thanes were royal officials. In return for the king granting them land, support and protection, or acknowledging their inherited rights to this, the elite gave the king their political, military and economic support, however nominal this might be in practice. This network of royal officials or people submitting allegiance to the kings was essential. Power flowed into their hands (and on to the king) by means of a highly structured and organized landscape of agricultural exploitation. Power bases, which leaders used both to protect themselves and to demonstrate their status and authority, were primarily bases for the collection, transformation and redistribution of tax and tribute. Kings regularly toured their kingdoms and visited these centres (and their resident officials) in order to physically reinforce their presence, to exert relations of

control and clientship, and to collect tribute. Surplus resources, both in terms of people and materials, were used to support a range of specialized activities and to control the production and/or distribution of prestige goods, which could be used to both create and reinforce social positions and promote political alliances. But power remained highly devolved and there was always the danger that local leaders might use the considerable power which they possessed to oppose their overlords, particularly when Pictland was too large and diverse an area to be easily managed (see below).

In many respects the Church fulfilled a similar role to the secular elite, as sympathetic landowners who strove to support the system which provided them with the resources to live and undertake their missionary work. But in addition, and most importantly, they provided ideological sanction and legitimization for the kings and nobility. Indeed, the introduction of Christianity is likely to have been the biggest force for change in the early historic period. With Christianity the character of kingship was revolutionized. The Church influenced how kings were chosen and strove to introduce a more peaceful society in which there was no place for the aggression of petty kings.

Whether as clients of the nobility or Church, the majority of the population continued, throughout this period, to provide the agricultural wealth from which royal authority was ultimately derived. At the local level the nature of lordship obviously changed, and they would presumably have been aware of owing allegiance to an overking whom they might never see. Through the missionary activities of the Church their expectations of life, society and authority would also gradually have been reshaped.

Deciding whether Pictland had developed into a State is rather an invidious exercise, given that so many possible definitions exist for this term. That said, it is not inappropriate to acknowledge that Pictland possessed many of the attributes of an early State: power was clearly highly devolved but, none the less, Pictland was a definite territory with demarcated divisions, which were administered by 'institutions' who attempted to ensure that there was centralized control of resources and military force; there were probably full-time specialists, society was highly stratified, people owed tribute and military service and use was made of literacy, even if exploitation of its full potential was yet to materialize.

## When?

Clearly the advent of Pictish symbols implies an element of political and ideological cohesion throughout much of Pictland. But whether these originate in the late sixth century (at the time of Bridei mac Máelchú), late seventh century (at the time of Bridei mac Bile), or even later, the clearest

indications of Pictish political consolidation began with the introduction of the Roman Church in the early eighth century. The clear inference is that the Church was exerting a considerable influence on Pictland, and the ambitions of its active clergy were closely integrated with the political aspirations of the social elite.

Further direct evidence for the advent of political consolidation could, in theory, be sought from the evolution/introduction of the sophisticated divisions of land and associated administration which developed in Pictland. The creation of the post of thane marks a crucial stage in the development of society when, due to the expansion of their territories, kings were no longer considered part of one's extended family. Although much of the evidence for thanes is later in date, the post, if not the terminology, undoubtedly originates during the Pictish period. The large number of later thanages at places with pre-Celtic names implies a pre-ninth-century origin, and it is tempting to assume that many Class II sculpted stones were being erected at the religious and/or secular centres of these land units.

The historian Michael Lynch, in his book *Scotland: A New History*, prefers to see the process of consolidation (which was certainly not unilinear) beginning with the reign of Constantín mac Fergusa in 789. In terms of links with Argyll, this is certainly the case, although the Picts and Dál Riata had been gradually coming together for some time beforehand: the Pictish king Óengus (729–61) had Dál Riata blood in him. Between 789 and 842, after which Cináed mac Ailpín seized power, there had already been three kings of Fortriu who were Gaels by origin and who ruled both kingdoms for part, if not all, of their reigns. Cináed mac Ailpín, like some of his Pictish predecessors, also adopted the practice of giving his sons alternately Pictish and Dál Riata names, which is indicative of both political sensitivities and reality.

We need not doubt that the Pictish kingdom was at its greatest extent during the eighth century, before the Viking incursions had begun to nibble away at its edges. By this time it had also reached a high level of maturity and sophistication. Not least, it had its own head church at St Andrews (founded between 729 and 747). Clearly a very wealthy foundation, the mainstream European aspirations of the Pictish kings are exemplified in the St Andrews sarcophagus (see **colour plate 12**), testimony to a vibrant native Church. In addition, the range and proliferation of later carved stones testify not simply to the wealth of the kingdom, but to its new-found security in the arms of the Church.

## Where?

In the time of Bridei mac Máelchú the Pictish power base was clearly in the north, but by the seventh century Fortrenn (Fortriu), in the Fife/Perthshire area of Scotland, had come to predominate. The continued importance of what had been the base of the fourth-century Verturiones need not surprise us, given the agricultural wealth of this area. Such abundance may have precipitated the need for more complex mechanisms to accommodate its exploitation. Furthermore, this was an area where the Church had a presence from an early (sub-Roman) date. Fortriu was to become synonymous with the Pictish nation from the late seventh century onwards.

## Cináed mac Ailpín

Cináed mac Ailpín's background is rather obscure, although he was probably related to the Cenél nGabhráin. King of Argyll (840–2), like his predecessors he sought, and ultimately obtained, the 'prize' of Pictland. Undoubtedly the agricultural wealth of Pictland was an enormous temptation to power-hungry warlords, but he may also have been impelled to move east due to the pressure of Viking attacks on Argyll, which also blocked him from moving north and cut the Dál Riata off from their Irish homeland. In this he was helped by the fact

that many of the Pictish nobles had already been wiped out by the Vikings in 839; the tradition that he was personally responsible for the treacherous death of the Pictish nobility at a feast in Scone is likely to be fictitious. None the less, despite the apparent power vacuum, there was obviously local resistance to his leadership (four Pictish kings are named during the early years of his leadership), which was not successfully eradicated until 848.

Cináed mac Ailpín chose to cultivate the Pictish centre at Scone to become his new royal centre and inauguration site (perhaps bringing to it the 'Stone of Destiny') and invested the church at Dunkeld with some of St Columba's relics. In doing so he was affirming the extension of his authority into the heartland of Pictland. His choice of Dunkeld is a reflection of its long-standing significance as an early historic power centre (probably sited at King's Seat) and its earlier significance as a prehistoric tribal centre (if the derivation of its name, 'fortress of the Caledones' is any guide). The presence of well-established Gaelic settlement in this area may also be relevant, for the area appears to have been subject to considerable migration since at least 739 when *Athfotla,* 'new Ireland', is first referred to.

At this time, Cináed's leadership was probably not considered any more unusual than some of his predecessors. Why then are all Scottish kings numbered from him, and why does he tend to be credited with laying the foundations of the modern Scottish nation? The answer lies in the fact, as could only be recognized later, that he was the founder of the first Scottish royal dynasty. Not only did his sons succeed him but, after a minor break between 878 and 889, the family line was continued by alternating kingship between a small kin group. This transformation in modes of inheritance marks a distinct break with past practice where inheritance had been determined from within a larger eligible kin group. That this change was accepted, may be largely due to the influence of the Church (see

Chapter 3). Modern historians now recognize the events of *c*. 900 as being the more important landmark than the event of 842. So, although the significance of Cináed mac Ailpín in the origins of the Scottish nation is now diminished, his special place in history rests on the fact that he was recognized shortly afterwards as being the founder of the dynasty which had made Alba its own.

## The birth of *Alba*

Around 900 the territorial term 'Alba' was first coined to replace the people-based term 'Pictland', which had continued in use *after* the accession of Cináed mac Ailpín. In doing so, it expressed a new type of nation and a more territorial notion of kingship. Domnall mac Constantín (Donald II; 889–900) became the first person to be described as 'king of Alba' and his was also the last reign in which the *Old Scottish Chronicle* referred to *Pictavia*. Subsequently the Pictish king-list was expanded to include a foundation legend which described the origin of the seven kingdoms of Pictland. There is no mention of Argyll, or the areas by then under Viking domination, and this appears to be an explicit effort to create a tradition that the Picts had, from the beginning, lived in a unified territory, a conscious attempt to assert the new form of dynastic succession and kingship. Such blatant manipulation of genealogies as a means of expressing a political situation is not new, but this is an early example of how the mac Ailpín dynasty (848–1034) was to exploit literacy to shape its new image. The importance of literacy had clearly been recognized by the early state of *Alba*, and was being used to full effect.

The major suppression of characteristic Pictish activities may relate to the same period although, again, the process had begun much earlier. A late reference in the *Old Scottish Chronicle* states that 'the Gaels, with their king [Domnall; 858–62], at Forteviot, made rights and laws of the kingdom of Aed of Eochaid', referring to an

eighth-century king under whom the Dál Riata had obtained their independence from the Picts. The more significant event probably took place in 906, when King Constantín mac Áeda (Constantine II) and Bishop Cellach 'and the Scots likewise, upon the hill of Faith near the royal city of Scone, swore to preserve the laws and disciplines of the Faith and the rights in church and gospels'. This was a very significant gesture, although it is unclear whether specific laws (*leges Kenneth Macalpinae*, mentioned in the thirteenth century) are actually being referred to. If so, this would have been unusual at this time although, in any case, it was the physical gesture of the promulgation which would have been most significant.

## Scottish identity

With the apparent disregard for Pictish characteristics and the conscious coining of a new name for the kingdom, it becomes appropriate for the first time for us to refer to both the Gaelic and Pictish inhabitants of *Alba* as Scots. Contemporary literature refers to them as *fir Alban*, 'men of Scotland' and the historian Dauvit Broun believes that the first people who thought of themselves as 'Scots' in any way ancestral to the sense we use today were, therefore, the tenth-century Gaelic speakers of *Alba*.

## What happened to the Pictish identity?

The term 'Picts' was used only in foreign sources until 918. According to later sources, the Picts were totally wiped out (Declaration of Arbroath 1320), ousted from their heritage (*Old Scottish Chronicle*) and their language disappeared (Henry of Huntingdon, *History of the English*). It is true that the Pictish language did indeed disappear, and this is likely to have been the culmination of a process which began well before 789 when the presence of migrants, Dál Riata overlords and clerics would gradually have eroded its general currency. Yet its final demise was not simply the result of an overhaul of the nobility. It is likely to have been exacerbated by a combination of the social and economic upheavals which followed in the wake of frequent Viking attacks and the aggression of a revitalized Gaelic Church, promoting the language of St Columba. Similarly, the practice of using Pictish symbols on sculpture was already in decline from the mid-eighth century, and was obviously not adopted by the Gaels for whom the symbolism had no direct relevance and indeed may have been inimical to their political existence. On the other hand, it cannot be proven whether Pictish manuscripts, if they existed in any large number, were consciously destroyed at this time, as has also been suggested.

The Picts themselves had not disappeared, but their identity was subsumed under the new terminology of *Alba* – they had become Scots. But while the Pictish identity might have been eradicated, their legacy was not. It was in fact the Dál Riata kingship which disappeared, not the Pictish one. Furthermore, there were aspects of Pictish culture which were adopted by the Scots. Foremost was their form of land organization, which alone suggests considerable continuity in the population at large.

In addition, the primacy of St Andrews, the head Church of Pictland, was not eclipsed, despite the increasing importance of Dunkeld. Probably founded in the reign of Óengus (729–61), Cellach, its bishop in 906, was apparently chief bishop of the whole nation, a pre-eminence which St Andrews appears to have retained.

## Extent of *Alba*

The extent of Pictland was curtailed by Viking incursions into Shetland, Orkney, the Western Isles and ultimately Caithness and Sutherland, but the disruption caused by these may, in fact, have provided the opportunity for the introduction of a new political structure. By the time *Alba* was coined, the term therefore could only have applied to a restricted part of former Pictland, perhaps just the region between the Spey, Forth and Druim Alban, an area comparable in size to other early historic kingdoms. Moray, which during Cináed mac Ailpín's reign had come under the domination of the Loairn dynasty who had expanded up the Great Glen, was probably virtually independent, under the authority of its own kings or *mormaer*. This independence started to lead to problems from the mid-tenth century, culminating in the short-lived takeover of Scotland by Macbethad mac Findlaích (Macbeth; 1040–57), *mormaer* of Moray, an event later immortalized by William Shakespeare.

Sueno's stone may have been erected as a memorial to one of the conflicts between the Scots and the men of Moray. The association of the stone with a king Sueno (Svein Forkbeard, a Danish king of both England and Denmark who died in 1014) was invented by early antiquarians. Scotland's tallest cross-slab – more than 6.5m (21ft) in height – was discovered in the eighteenth century. On one side is a long panel with a cross (**85**), much of which is filled with fine interlace. Beneath this is a panel with opposed figures, to which we shall return. On the sides are panels of inhabited vine scroll, a distinctive form of decoration which the Picts adopted from the Northumbrians. The opposite side is divided into four panels, each of which is crowded with scenes from a battle, with rows of regimented foot-soldiers, archers, horsemen and the lines of slain and beheaded warriors (see **82**).

The stone cannot be precisely dated, but probably belongs to somewhere from the mid-ninth century to the tenth. Radiocarbon dates from excavated timber sockets around its base, possibly for the scaffolding used to erect the weighty stone, broadly confirm this date-range and that the stone has been re-erected close to its original location.

If the battle is not imaginary and contrived solely to convey a series of Christian messages or a foundation legend, it may represent a real battle, most plausibly a conflict between Cináed mac Ailpín (or one of his descendants)

85 *Sueno's stone, west face.*

and the men of Moray, in which the Scots finally succeed in obtaining the submission of the men of Moray. An interpretation of the scene beneath the cross as the inauguration ceremony of a mac Ailpín king, surrounded by clerics (perhaps of St Andrews and Scone or Dunkeld), and/or St Andrew and St Columba in person, might support this theory. An alternative battle is the one fought by Dubh, one of Cináed mac Ailpín's successors, who was killed at Forres in 966. There is an early tradition that his body lay beneath the bridge at Kinloss prior to burial, and this bridge is perhaps depicted on the stone, with Dubh's head highlighted by a box around it.

Regardless of whether a real battle is depicted, this monument was created both to express thanks to God and to continually remind all those who viewed it of the authority of the Scottish king, as testified by his military might and the legitimization provided by the Church. Given the political volatility of this area, it is therefore not surprising that the stone should later have been deliberately buried (albeit very carefully since it was not broken) in order to suppress this message.

## What happened to Argyll?

That part of Argyll which was not overrun by the Scandinavians became known as *Gall Gaidel* and its absence from *Alba* is significant, since it presupposes that the new Scottish kings had virtually turned their backs on this area in the political sense, although they continued to bury their dead on Iona. Cináed mac Ailpín and his successors settled permanently in the east. Although the Argyll mainland was still occupied, activity on hilltop power centres was scaled down or abandoned. Iona, devastated by Viking raids in 795, had been largely abandoned in 807. However, some form of influential monastic community did continue on the island (86) and some of the mac Ailpín kings were probably buried there until 900, and again from the second half of the tenth

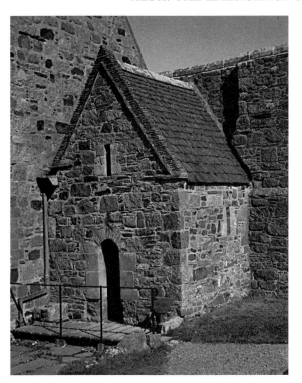

*86 St Columba's shrine, Iona. Unlikely to pre-date the ninth century at the earliest, this rebuilt chapel bears architectural similarities in proportion and style to Irish stone chapels now thought to be eleventh- or twelfth-century in date (David Breeze).*

century. Domnall Bán mac Donnchaba (Donald III, died 1097) was the last king to be buried there, by which time Iona had re-emerged as the centre for the *Gall Gaidel*. Later it became part of the Lordship of the Isles. The significance of this area for the Scottish nation was not forgotten. Writing in 1522, Hector Boece informs us in his *History of the Scots* that William Elphinstone, Bishop of Aberdeen (1483–1514), was concerned to search out 'the antiquities of the Scottish people, especially in the Hebrides, where are preserved the sepulchres of our ancient kings and the ancient monuments of our race'.

## *Alba* in Europe

The development of early Scotland was akin to parallel developments throughout much of western Europe, which saw the expansion and consolidation of kingdoms, and which were also forced to cope with Viking attacks. These kingdoms were also united by the presence of Christianity, a force whose religious and intellectual links cut across national boundaries and whose mobile clerics were highly efficient ambassadors for change, both in the political and religious sense.

Obviously it is impossible to perceive *Alba* as others perceived her. In fact it is surprising that her political precocity did not excite more comment. However, we can state with confidence that the technical, artistic, religious and administrative prowess of the Scots, Dál Riata and Picts was easily on a par with that of contemporary Europe. Many of their achievements were highly original, even if they had little immediate impact beyond northern Britain. At the same time, it was not inappropriate for the ninth *Commemoration Book of Durham* to juxtapose the name of Constantín mac Fergusa with that of Charlemagne, the much acclaimed emperor of the Carolingians. A quick glance at intermarriages in the family tree of the mac Ailpín dynasty is misleading, since it would appear to suggest that their interests were restricted to northern Britain. Yet this includes powerful and vibrant Scandinavian dynasties (at York and Dublin), who controlled the coastal waters of western Europe: *Alba* was thus a full participant in international contacts.

## Postscript: the kingdom comes of age

Constantín mac Áeda (900–43) consolidated the strength of the mac Ailpín dynasty and extended the geographical extent of *Alba* to include Lothian and Strathclyde through a process of military victories and intermarriage. Constantín was also a clever politician, skilfully manipulating the York and Dublin Danes against each other, which also spoiled the interests of ambitious kings of Wessex. The early tenth-century ruler of Bernicia may also have regarded himself as Constantín's tributary.

**87** *Brechin was founded by Cináed mac Máel-coluim (Kenneth II) between 971 and 995. The round tower, a feature of Irish monasteries, is a later feature, built between c. 1090 and 1130 (compare with the round tower at Abernethy). The roof was capped in the fourteenth century (RCAHMS).*

Thus, by the time he retired to the monastery of St Andrews in 943, the medieval kingdom of Scotland could be said to have come of age. Unfortunately the remaining years of the mac Ailpín dynasty (until 1034) are badly served by both archaeological evidence and historical sources, but by 1018 her southern boundaries had extended to the Solway and Tweed, more or less the limits of modern Scotland. Despite recurrent political crises as rival segments of the dynasty competed for power, and steady encirclement by Scandinavian powers, consolidation continued throughout this period. In particular, the Church went from strength to strength (87). Few of the early historic power bases survived to become modern centres (such as St Andrews) but we are beginning to pick up the origins of new urban centres. Perth, established close to the royal centre at Scone, was undoubtedly under royal authority and control from the beginning. The credit for much of this success lies in the groundwork of the Picts and Dál Riata whose strength, as the emergent nation of Scots, lay not only in their innovative qualities and unique achievements, but in the composite nature of their kingdoms.

One monument alone epitomizes the range of these achievements: the Dupplin cross (see **75**). Whether this ninth-century monument depicts Constantín mac Fergusa, 'king of Fortriu' (*c.* 789–820) and one of the first Gaels to rule both Pictland and Argyll, or a later Gaelic king, this monarch is proudly depicted as master of all he surveys: the Pictish agricultural heartland and the royal palace of Forteviot at its centre; at his feet the seriated ranks of his nobility and army. The symbiotic relationship between the Church and 'State' is testified by the juxtaposition of secular and ecclesiastical imagery, a relationship we must assume to have been reiterated in the monument's ogham and Latin texts. Finally, in his very name – Constantín – we find confirmation of the wider political and religious aspirations of an early historic king, whose political awareness and ambit extended well beyond the shores of *Alba*.

# Monuments and museums to visit

This list confines itself to sites which are publicly accessible; * indicates a charge. For opening times and admission charges for sites in Historic Scotland's care (**in bold**), telephone 0131-668-8600. For further information about other sites contact Tourist Information.

The numbers refer to the map (**88**). Further details of many of these sites can be found in the *Exploring Scotland's Heritage* series (HMSO and RCAHMS).

Class I refers to undressed stones with incised Pictish symbols; Class II refers to dressed stones with Pictish symbols and Christian iconography (see Chapter 5).

1   *Aberdeen: Anthropological Museum, Marishal College, Broad Street.*
Small display on Picts including Class I from Fairy Knowe.

2   ***Aberlemno*** (NO 522 558; NO 522 555).
Magnificent Class II stone with battle scene in churchyard; three stones nearby beside B9134.

3   ***Abernethy*** (NO 189 164).
Round tower at entrance to churchyard; Class I set at its base.

4   *Applecross* (NG 713 458).
Site of early monastery, includes several cross-slabs.

5   ***Ardestie souterrain*** (NO 502 344).

6   ***Brechin round tower*** (NO 596 601).
Late eleventh/early twelfth-century round tower, originally free-standing, now attached to the cathedral (which contains cross-slab from Aldbar, inscribed slab with Virgin Mary and eleventh-century hogback).

* 7   ***Broch of Gurness*** (HY 381 268).
Pictish house rebuilt to one side of the prehistoric remains. Small museum contains Class I.

8   ***Brough of Birsay*** (HY 239 285).
Pictish power centre, but most of visible structural remains are Norse and later.

9   ***Burghead well, King Street*** (NJ 111 691).
Remains of fort on headland to west. See also display in library window.

* 10   *Bute Museum, Stuart Street, Rothesay.*
Includes several early crosses.

11   *Canna* (NG 229 043; NG 269 055). National Trust for Scotland.
Early monastery at Sgòr nam Ban-Naomha and weathered, but impressive, cross at site of medieval chapel.

12   ***Carlungie souterrains*** (NO 511 359).

13   *Craig Phádraig* (NH 640 452). Forest Enterprise.
Iron Age fort reused by Picts.

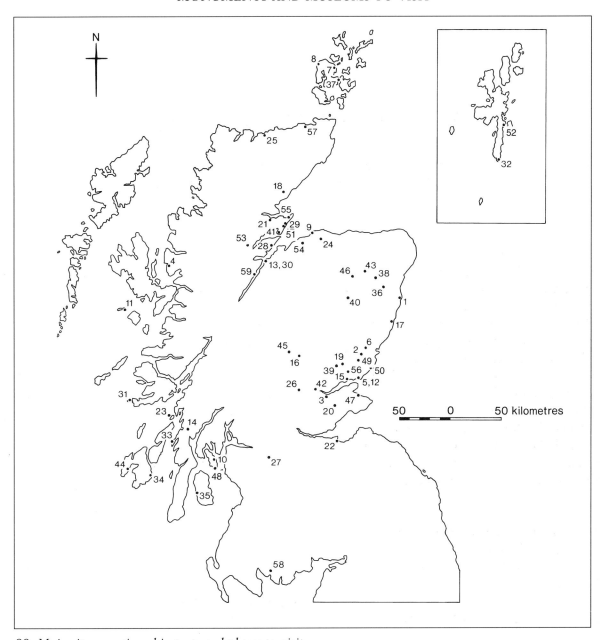

**88** *Main sites mentioned in text, and places to visit.*

**14 *Dunadd*** (NR 836 935).
Dál Riata power centre with carvings and inscription. See also carvings at **Kilmartin church** (NR 834 988).

**15 *Dundee: McManus Galleries, Albert Square.***
Contains variety of Pictish sculptures, including Benvie and reconstructed long-cist burial from Lundin Links.

**16 *Dunfallandy*** (NN 946 565).
Class II.

* **17 *Dunnottar*** (NO 881 838).
Medieval castle overlies what may have been Pictish power centre.

* 18 *Dunrobin Castle Museum, Sutherland* (NC 850 008).
Outstanding collection of 18 Pictish symbol stones, includes an example with ogham.

19 *Eassie* (NO 352 474).
Class II.

20 *East Lomond Hill, fort* (NO 244 062). Fife Regional Council.

21 *Edderton* (NH 719 842).
Eighth/ninth-century cross-slab near entrance to churchyard.

22 *Edinburgh: National Museum of Scotland, Queen Street* (moving to Chamber Street in 1998).
Large collection of early Christian carvings, including Hilton of Cadboll stone and Tarbat inscription. Holdings also include St Ninian's Isle treasure, Norrie's Law hoard, Monymusk reliquary, Hunterston brooch and finds from the Brough of Birsay and Dunadd.

23 *Eileach an Naoimh, Garvellachs* (NM 640 097).
Early monastery with well-preserved beehive cells.

* 24 *Elgin Cathedral* (NJ 221 630).
Medieval cathedral includes Pictish cross-slab. In addition, *Elgin Museum* has 17 sculpted stones on display, including shrine fragments from Kinnedar.

25 *Farr* (NC 714 622).
Fine ninth-century cross-slab in churchyard.

26 *Fowlis Wester* (NN 927 240).
Reconstruction of cross-slab in centre of village; original now moved into church, alongside a second slab found built into church fabric.

27 *Glasgow: Hunterian Museum, University Avenue.*
Finds from Dundurn, Dunollie and Dumbarton.

* 28 *Groam House Museum, High Street, Rosemarkie.*
Large collection of Pictish carvings, including impressive Class II originally from Rosemarkie church.

29 *Hilton of Cadboll, chapel* (NH 873 768).

30 *Inverness Museum and Art Gallery, Castle Wynd.*
Includes various Pictish stones, replica of Craig Phádraig hanging bowl and carved jet pendant.

31 *Iona* (NM 286 245).
Site of Columba's monastery with surviving vallum, series of splendid eighth-century high crosses and large collection of other carvings (in abbey museum and St Ronan's chapel).

32 *Jarlshof* (HU 399 096).
* Multi-period site includes possible Pictish buildings.

33 *Keills chapel* (NR 690 806).
Medieval chapel contains high cross, early medieval and later carvings.

34 *Kildalton, Islay* (NR 458 508).
Finest surviving high cross in Scotland. Cast in Kelvingrove Museum, Glasgow.

35 *King's Caves, Arran* (NR 884 309).
Walk from Forest Enterprise car-park near Blackwaterfoot. Cave (restricted access) contains many early Christian and later carvings, including ogham inscriptions.

36 *Kintore church* (NJ 793 162).
Class II.

* 37 *Kirkwall, Orkney: Tankerness House Museum, Broad Street.*
Includes finds from Gurness, Brough of Birsay, Buckquoy and various Pictish stones, including the Knowe of Burrian.

38 *Maiden stone* (NJ 703 247).
Class II.

\* 39 *Meigle* (NO 287 445).
Museum contains 25 Pictish carvings, one of the most notable assemblages of early historic sculpture in western Europe.

40 *Migvie* (NJ 436 068).
Class II.

41 *Nigg* (NH 804 717).
Ornate late eighth-century cross-slab.

42 *Perth Museums and Art Galleries, George Street.*
Includes sculpted stones from Inchyra, Gellyburn, St Madoes and New Scone.

43 *Picardy stone* (NJ 609 302).
Class I.

44 *Port Charlotte: Museum of Islay Life.*
Large collection of early carvings.

45 *Queen's View, ring-fort* (NN 863 601). Forest Enterprise.

46 *Rhynie Old Churchyard* (NJ 499 265).
Two Class I.

\* 47 *St Andrews Cathedral* (NO 513 166).
Museum includes sarcophagus and other carvings.

48 *St Blane's, Bute* (NS 094 534).
Twelfth-century Romanesque church, site of St Blane's monastery. Includes early gravestones and the 'cauldron', possibly an early Christian building.

49 *St Orland's stone* (NO 400 500).
Class II includes carving of boat.

50 *St Vigean's, Arbroath* (NO 638 429).
Museum contains 32 Pictish carvings.

51 *Shandwick* (NH 855 747).
Tall and very impressive Class II, late eighth- or ninth- century.

52 *Shetland Museum, Lower Hillhead, Lerwick.*
Includes sculpted stones from Papil and Mail.

53 *Strathpeffer* (NH 485 585).
Class I.

54 *Sueno's stone* (NJ 046 595).
The tallest medieval sculpture in Scotland, depicting, among other things, a series of battle scenes.

55 *Tarbat, Portmahomack* (NH 914 840).
Display in church includes some of the carved stones which suggest that this was the site of an important monastery.

56 *Tealing souterrain* (NO 412 381).

\* 57 *Thurso Heritage Museum, High Street.*
Includes two Pictish slabs.

58 *Trusty's Hill, Anwoth* (NX 588 560).
Pictish carvings carved on living rock by entrance to fort, perhaps evidence for a Pictish raiding party.

\* 59 *Urquhart Castle* (NH 531 286).
Medieval castle overlies Pictish power centre.

*Note Meffan Institute, Forfar* (NO 455 505)
This reopened in March 1995. It includes sculpted stones from Kirriemuir, Menmuir and Wester Denoon, beautifully displayed.

# Further reading

## Early historic texts

*Adomnan's Life of Columba*, ed. A.O. Anderson and M.O. Anderson, Oxford, 1991.

*Adomnán of Iona: Life of St Columba,* trans. R. Sharpe, Harmondsworth, 1995.

*Senchus fer nAlban*, ed. J. Bannerman, in *Studies in the History of Dal Riada*, Edinburgh, 1974.

*Historia Ecclesiastica Gentis Anglorum*, trans. L. Sherley-Price, rev. R.E. Latham as *Bede: Ecclesiastical History of the English People*, Harmondsworth, 2nd rev. edn, 1990.

## Sources for sculpture, manuscripts and metalwork

Allen, J.R. and Anderson, J. *The Early Christian Monuments of Scotland*, Edinburgh, 1903 (repr. 1993 by Pinkfoot Press, Balgavies, Angus).

Henderson, G. *From Durrow to Kells: the Insular Gospel Books 650–800*, London, 1987.

Ritchie, A. *Picts,* Edinburgh, 1989.

Royal Commission on the Ancient and Historical Monuments of Scotland *Pictish Symbol Stones: a hand-list 1994.*

Spearman. R.M. and Higgitt, J. (eds) *The Age of Migrating Ideas*, Edinburgh, 1993.

Youngs, S. (ed.) *'The Work of Angels': masterpieces of Celtic metalwork, 6th–9th centuries AD*, London, 1989.

## History, language and place-names

Broun, D. 'The origin of Scottish identity' in C. Bjørn, A. Grant and K.J. Stringer (eds) *Nations, Nationalism and Patriotism in the European Past*, Copenhagen, 1994, pp. 35-55.

Forsyth, K. 'Language in Pictland, spoken and written' in E. Nicoll (ed.) *A Pictish Panorama*, Balgavies, Angus, 1995.

Lynch, M. *Scotland: A New History*, London, 1992.

Nicolaisen, W.F.H. *Scottish Place-names*, London, 1986.

Smyth, A.P. *Warlords and Holymen: Scotland AD 80–1000*, London, 1984.

## Specialist works on the Picts, Gaels and Scots

Nicoll, E. (ed.) *A Pictish Panorama*, Balgavies, Angus, 1995 (contains a Select Bibliography of Works Relating to the Picts, compiled by Dr Jack R.F. Burt, which includes the following recommended publications):

Alcock, L. 'Early historic fortifications in Scotland' in G. Guilbert (ed.) *Hill-fort Studies*, London, 1981, pp. 150–80.

Alcock, L. 'The activities of potentates in Celtic Britain, AD 500–800: a positivist approach' in S.T. Driscoll and M.R. Nieke (eds) *Power and Politics in Early Medieval Britain and Ireland*, Edinburgh, 1988, pp. 22–46.

Alcock, L. *The Neighbours of the Picts: Angles, Britons and Scots at war and at home*, Dornoch, 1993.

Alcock, L. et al. 'Reconnaissance excavations on early historic fortifications at Dunollie, Dundurn, Alt Clut, Urquhart and Forteviot', *Proceedings of the Society of Antiquaries of Scotland*, 117 (1987), 119 (1989), 120 (1990) and 122 (1992).

Anderson, M.O. *Kings and Kingship in Early Scotland*, Edinburgh, 1980.

Anderson, M.O. 'Dalriada and the creation of the kingdom of the Scots' in D. Whitelock, R. Mckitterick and D. Dumville (eds) *Ireland in Early Mediaeval Europe*, Cambridge, 1982, pp. 106–32.

Armit, I. (ed.) *Beyond the Brochs*, Edinburgh, 1991.

Campbell, E. 'The archaeological evidence for contacts: imports, trade and economy in Celtic Britain AD 400-800' in K.R. Dark (ed.) *External Contacts and the Economy of Late Roman and Post-Roman Britain*, Woodbridge, 1996, pp. 83–96.

Campbell, J. *Bede's Reges and Principes*, Jarrow Lecture, 1979.

Charles-Edwards, T. 'Early medieval kingships in the British Isles' in S. Bassett (ed.) *The Origins of Anglo-Saxon Kingdoms*, Leicester, 1989, pp. 28–39.

Crawford, B.E. (ed.) *Scotland in Dark Age Europe*, St Andrews, 1994.

Driscoll, S.T. 'Power and authority in early historic Scotland: Pictish stones and other documents' in J. Gledhill, B. Bender and M. Larsen (eds) *State and Society: the emergence and development of social hierarchy and political centralisation*, London, 1988, pp. 215–36.

Driscoll, S.T. 'The archaeology of state formation in Scotland' in W.S. Hanson and E.A. Slater (eds) *Scottish Archaeology: new perceptions*, Aberdeen, 1991, pp. 81–111.

Driscoll, S.T. and Nieke, M.R. (eds) *Power and Politics in Early Medieval Britain and Ireland*, Edinburgh, 1988.

Friell, J.G.P. and Watson, W.G. (eds) *Pictish Studies: settlement, burial and art in Dark Age northern Britain*, Oxford, 1984.

Henderson, I. 'The "David Cycle" in Pictish Art' in J. Higgitt (ed.) *Early Medieval Sculpture in Britain and Ireland*, Oxford, 1986, pp. 87–123.

Hughes, K. *Celtic Britain in the Early Middle Ages*, Woodbridge, 1980.

Jackson, A. *The Symbol Stones of Scotland*, Kirkwall, 1984.

Lamb, R. 'Carolingian Orkney and its transformation' in C.E. Batey, J. Jesch and C.D. Morris (eds) *The Viking Age in Caithness, Orkney and the North Atlantic*, Edinburgh, 1994, pp. 260–71.

Macquarrie, A. 'Early Christian religious houses in Scotland: foundation and function' in J. Blair and R. Sharpe (eds) *Pastoral Care before the Parish*, Leicester, 1992.

Nieke, M.R. 'Settlement patterns in the first millennium AD: a case study of the island of Islay' in M. Chapman and H. Mytum (eds) *Settlement in North Britain, 1000 BC–AD 1000*, Oxford, 1983, pp. 299–325.

Nieke, M.R. 'Literacy and power: the introduction and use of writing in early historic Scotland' in J. Gledhill, B. Bender and M. Larsen (eds) *State and Society: the emergence and development of social hierarchy and political centralisation*, London, 1988, pp. 237–52.

Nieke, M.R. 'Penannular and related brooches: secular ornament or symbol in action' in R.M. Spearman and J. Higgitt (eds) *The Age of Migrating Ideas*, Edinburgh, 1993, pp. 128–34.

Samson, R. 'The reinterpretation of the Pictish symbols', *Journal of the British Archaeological Association*, 145 (1992), pp. 29–65.

Sellar, W.D.H. (ed.) *Moray: province and people*, Edinburgh, 1993.

Small, A. (ed.) *The Picts: a new look at old problems*, Dundee, 1987.

Thomas, C. *Christianity in Roman Britain to AD 500*, London, 1981.

Thomas, C. '"Gallici Nautae de Galliarum Provinciis" – sixth/seventh-century trade with Gaul, reconsidered', *Medieval Archaeology*, 34 (1990), pp. 1–26.

Wainwright, F.T. (ed.) *The Problem of the Picts*, Perth, 1955 (repr. 1980).

# Glossary

**barrow**  An earthen burial mound.

**broch**  Monumental, stone-built roundhouse constructed around 2000 years ago, with notable architectural details such as intramural cells and at least one upper storey or gallery.

**C-14**  see **radiocarbon dating**

**cist (long or short)**  A stone-lined and capped rectangular tomb.

**crannog**  Offshore (usually loch-side) structure, built of wood and stone, with houses and other buildings on it.

**crop mark**  Buildings and structures which have been ploughed flat leaving no visible traces at ground-level. In favourable conditions sub-surface features, e.g. ditches, may be visible due to differential rates of crop growth (or drying of soil).

**dendrochronology**  A means of dating based on the identification, counting and comparison of annual growth rings in ancient wood.

**dun**  Thick, stone-walled enclosure, usually sub-circular in plan, often likely to have been roofed, and interpreted as a defensive farmstead.

**Easter Tables**  Tables used by the Church to calculate the correct date for Easter (which varies) over a number of years.

**escutcheon**  Shield-shaped applied ornament, often doubling as the means by which a handle can be attached to the object.

**food renders**  Consumable taxes given by clients to their lords.

**henge**  A monument constructed in the late Neolithic/early Bronze Age (about 4500 years ago): sacred spaces were defined by circular banks with internal ditches and at least one entrance.

**Indo-European**  The name given to a family of languages which spread throughout Europe and much of southern Asia during early prehistory. Finnish, Basque and Estonian are the only surviving non-Indo-European languages in modern Europe.

**Insular art**  A style of art which developed in Ireland, Scotland and Northumbria during the early historic period. Sometimes also referred to as 'Hiberno-Saxon'.

**Iron Age**  In Scottish terms, the period from *c.* 600 BC to AD 1000; the Late Iron Age (AD 400–1000) is also known as the early historic period.

**material culture**  The physical remains from the past (artefacts, buildings, etc.) as studied, characterized and interpreted by archaeologists.

**matrilineal succession** Inheritance passed to males through the female line.

**midden** Rubbish-heap.

**mormaer** Ruler of a province.

**Mounth** The traditional boundary between the northern and southern Picts, as broadly defined by the Grampian mountains.

**radiocarbon dating (C-14)** A means of dating based on measuring the proportions of the C14 to C12 isotopes in organic matter. These results can be calibrated to produce a calendrical date-range, although variable rates of certainty have to be attached to these.

**ring-fort** Thick, stone-walled enclosure, usually sub-circular in plan, unlikely to have been roofed.

**soil mark** see **crop mark.**

**souterrain** Semi-subterranean, passage-like structure, usually constructed of stone and associated with above-ground houses.

**thanage** District of land administered by a thane, appointed to do so on behalf of a king or mormaer.

**thermoluminescence dating (TL)** A means of dating the firing of clay or burning of rocks or deposition of sediments. It is based on measuring luminescence generated in minerals by long-term exposure to natural background radiation, and the strengths of background sources in the sample and its deposition environment. Results are expressed as absolute or calendrical ages. Uncertainties vary from ± 5–10 per cent of age.

**timber-laced** A form of stone or earthen rampart construction in which a timber frame is constructed internally to provide additional strength. If this is burnt at high temperatures (over 1000 °C) the stone may fuse and become distorted (vitrified).

**vallum** A rampart - with associated ditch(es).

**vitrification** see **timber-laced.**

**votive deposits** Ritual offerings made to the gods.

**wheelhouse** An Iron Age sub-circular dry-stone building, the roof of which is supported by radial dry-stone piers (like the spokes of a wheel). Found in Shetland and the Western Isles.

# Index

# INDEX

INDEX